LEARN SQUASH
IN A WEEKEND

LEARN SQUASH
IN A WEEKEND

JAHANGIR KHAN
with KEVIN PRATT

Photography by Matthew Ward

RD PRESS

A DORLING KINDERSLEY BOOK

Art Editor Alison Donovan
Editor Deborah Opoczynska
Senior Art Editor Amanda Lunn
Series Editors Jo Weeks, Laura Harper
Deputy Art Director Tina Vaughan
Deputy Editorial Director Jane Laing
Production Controller Helen Creeke

First published in Australia in 1993 by RD Press
a registered business name of
Reader's Digest (Australia) Pty Limited
26-32 Waterloo Street, Surry Hills, NSW 2010

The National Library of Australia Cataloguing-in-Publication data

Khan, Jahangir.
    Learn squash in a weekend.

    Includes index.
    ISBN 0 86438 461 0.
    ISBN 0 86438 202 2 (series).

    1. Squash rackets (Game).
    (Series: Learn in a weekend series).

796.343

Computer page make-up by
Cloud 9 Designs, Hampshire, UK
Reproduced by Colourscan, Singapore
Printed and bound by
Arnoldo Mondadori, Verona, Italy

CONTENTS

INTRODUCTION

SQUASH IS MY LIFE. Ever since I was a boy in Pakistan, all I have wanted to do is hit that little ball around the court. I came to England and set out to fulfil my ambition: to become the best player in the world. In 1981, when I was 17, my dream came true: I won the World Open Final against my old rival, Geoff Hunt. From there, I went on to maintain the longest unbeaten run in the history of the game – five years, seven months, and one day. After many years at the pinnacle of my sport, I still love playing squash; there is always something new to learn in practice; there is always a new limit to aim for in training; and there is always a new challenge with every opponent. The rules are easy to learn and you can very quickly start playing enjoyable, competitive games with players of your own standard. If you join a club, you will be able to take part in competitions and improve

THE WINNER
Winner of ten British Opens, six World Championships, and numerous other competitions throughout the globe, Jahangir Khan will go down in history as the best squash player of all time.

your ability by taking on players of higher standards. This book shows you how to master the rudiments of the game over the course of a weekend, right from the basics of hitting the ball correctly, through the subtleties of match-winning technique to the exercise it takes to acquire the necessary level of fitness. It will also serve as an invaluable source of reference as you hone your squash skills in the years to come. There are now 15 million people around the world who play regularly, so you are about to learn one of the most popular sports of the day. I hope this book sets you on the path toward a life-long love of squash. No matter what your age, if you are enthusiastic and apply a little dedication, you are sure to be enriched, both physically and mentally by this wonderful game.

JAHANGIR KHAN

PREPARING FOR THE WEEKEND

Get the most from your Weekend Course by preparing in advance

YOU WILL LEARN MORE, and have greater fun, if you plan your weekend in advance. Arrange to have a court at your disposal by hiring one from a local club or recreation centre. If possible, find a partner who is as keen to learn as you are. Make sure you have the right equipment, including proper squash shoes, kit, racket, and balls. Take up a fitness programme before you start playing. There is an old squash saying that is worth remembering: "Get fit to play squash; don't play squash to get fit". Study the rules of the game (see p.17) so that you have a basic understanding of how squash is played before you even set foot on the court. Familiarize yourself with the court markings and the basic positions, such as where to serve from, where to receive the serve, and where to stand during a **rally**. Get used to holding your racket with the

SQUASH KIT

Invest in a good-quality squash kit, including on-court wear and a tracksuit. Trainers or tennis shoes are no substitute for a good pair of squash shoes.

• *Choose the speed of ball suited to you*

RACKETS & BALLS

Find a racket that feels just right for you – neither too heavy nor too light. Make sure the grip is comfortable. Buy a selection of fast and slow balls, so that you can determine which is best suited to your style of play.

• *Buy proper squash shoes*

• *Store equipment in a kit bag*

Make sure the • grip is comfortable

• *Use wraps to make the grip more secure*

YOU WILL LEARN MORE, and have greater fun, if you plan your weekend in advance. Arrange to have a court at your disposal by hiring one from a local club or recreation centre. If possible, find a partner who is as keen to learn as you are. Make sure you have the right equipment, including proper squash shoes, kit, racket, and balls. Take up a fitness programme before you start playing. There

9.7m (32ft)

1.6m (5ft 2in)

4.3m (14ft)

6.4m (21ft)

1.7m (5ft 5in)

• Learn the rules about swings

COURT DIMENSIONS
You will be able to develop a good feel for the dimensions of a squash court simply by walking around one. Take some time to watch how the other players position themselves and move around the court while playing.

RULES OF THE GAME
Learn the rules about **obstruction** and illegal racket swings. This will help to ensure that you have a safe and enjoyable game, and that you do not lose it merely through default.

• Look straight ahead

WARMING UP ON-COURT
Go through a number of exercises on the court to thoroughly warm your muscles. This will help you to avoid any muscle injuries and soreness.

WARMING UP OFF-COURT
Before you set foot on the court, ensure that your muscles are prepared for the game by taking up regular exercise in a gym or other spacious area.

• Exercise to improve strength and stamina

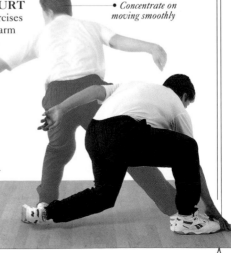

• Concentrate on moving smoothly

SQUASH KIT

"Dress well, play well" is a good rule for squash players to follow

SQUASH IS A FAST AND VIGOROUS GAME, not a fashion parade, but it is important to have the right attitude to the kit you wear. By playing in shabby or dirty clothes, you are showing a lack of respect for your opponent, for yourself, and for the sport. Smart, clean clothes show your regard for the game and that you are taking matters seriously. Shorts, skirts, and shirts must be able to stretch to allow you to reach for the ball; avoid materials that soak up perspiration. Keep a towel on-court to dry yourself. Put money and valuables in your kit bag and place it close to the front wall. It is essential to wear a good pair of squash shoes to help movement and reduce the risk of slips and injury.

OFF-COURT WEAR

What you wear before and after your game is almost as important as what you wear on-court. A tracksuit will keep you warm while you loosen your muscles before playing, and while you warm down after the game. You may choose to wear your tracksuit to the court, but don't put it back on over your squash clothes after playing – wet clothes will give you a chill. Never wear your squash shoes off the court – it ruins the sole.

• **MATERIAL**
Choose a tracksuit made of a flexible, warm material, that allows you to ease and stretch muscles without the risk of "cold-start" injuries.

TRACKSUIT
Always wear your tracksuit to warm up in before starting the game. This helps to avoid injuries on-court and unnecessary stiffness the day after.

KIT BAG
Buy a large bag with compartments for valuables, clothes, wet kit, towels, toiletries, rackets, and balls.

ON-COURT WEAR

Clothes should be comfortable and clean, to help you feel fresh and ready for a good game. Wear light colours so that the ball stands out clearly against you. Remove any items of jewellery that might cause injury to yourself or, more likely, to your opponent. Only put your squash shoes on once on the court.

• SHIRT
A short-sleeved shirt with an open neck allows freedom of movement. Wear it neatly tucked in.

SHORTS •
A fast game of squash involves many strides and leaps. Wear shorts that stretch to avoid embarrassing splits.

• SKIRTS
Women should wear skirts that allow easy movement, but are long enough to deter any unwanted scrutiny.

UNDERWEAR
Underwear is important if you are to be comfortable on-court. Men should wear a support, and women will need a well-fitting sports bra. Unsuitable garments may cause discomfort and distract you from the game.

• SOCKS
Good socks protect against blisters. Avoid cheap or ill-fitting pairs that will aggravate weakened skin.

SHOES

The correct shoes are essential. Invest in a pair of squash shoes, rather than relying on standard trainers or tennis shoes. The grip, heel, and ankle support are different on a squash shoe and make a significant difference in terms of performance as well as of the risk of injury. Make sure the soles of the shoes are non-marking. Wear new shoes around the house to break them in and help to avoid blisters. Tie laces so that they never touch the ground, otherwise you are quite likely to take a trip.

Shoes with a herring-bone-grip sole will help you to turn and push off quickly

The heel of the shoe should be no more than 3cm (1.25in) in depth

RACKETS & BALLS

Choose the ball and racket that feel best for you

GREAT ADVANCES HAVE BEEN MADE in squash-racket technology. Originally made of wood with animal-gut strings, there was little to distinguish one racket from another, but today's rackets are made of graphite with synthetic strings and have various shaped heads. They can present a bewildering choice to the beginner. There are four types of ball, each suited to different levels and styles of play.

RACKETS

Choose a racket that feels right. If it is cumbersome, it is too heavy. If it feels like a feather, it is too light. Try out several until you shake hands with the one for you. The most expensive racket is a waste of money at this stage, since only a good player can take advantage of it. The cheapest ones are made of inferior materials, and can smash easily. Ask other players what they recommend.

VIBRATION
A great force is generated when you strike the ball and some of it shoots down the racket and into your arm. A **vibration absorber** (above), placed in the centre of the racket face, helps to lessen this effect.

• *Vibration absorber*

Small round head •

Large oval head •

HEAD •
Regardless of the size of the head, the best way to hit the ball is in the centre of the racket face. A larger head is not necessarily an advantage, but may provide the beginner with extra confidence.

SHAFT •
Graphite rackets are stronger than wood, which is important when you hit the wall instead of the ball, but the shaft is still vulnerable, so avoid undue strain.

Open-throat head •

• STRINGS
When racket strings break, they can easily be replaced. Some players insist on gut because it gives more "spin", but it is not as hard-wearing as nylon.

prince

- *Very slow: for matches*

- *Slow: for practice*

Yellow dot

White dot

- *Medium: for beginners*

- *Fast: for novices*

Red dot

Blue dot

BALLS

Squash balls are hollow. When used, they become warm and the air inside expands, making them more bouncy. The better you are, the slower the ball you should use. If you use a ball that is too fast to start off with, it will become so bouncy that good squash becomes impossible. Use the blue- and red-dot balls to begin with; you can graduate to the white and yellow ones as you begin to gain confidence.

RACKET COVERS

Most rackets come with a cover, but buy one if yours did not. The cover will prevent the frame from being scuffed and the strings from breakage. It will also protect your racket against the elements – rain, which damages strings, and excessive cold, which can seriously weaken the shaft.

SECURITY

The best place to keep your squash rackets and balls is in your cover. For security, attach your name and address to it in case you lose it.

- *Single-racket cover*

- *Multi-racket bag*

GRIPS

Towelling	*Grips made of suede or towelling absorb moisture, but wear easily*	
Leather	*A leather grip will wear well, but tends to become very wet as you play*	
Synthetic	*Synthetic grips are durable, but tend to be slippery and can be difficult to grip*	

Rackets have suede, towelling, leather, or synthetic grips. Suede and towelling grips absorb moisture but wear easily. Leather wears well but can become wet as you perspire. Synthetics are also long-lasting but tend to have a slippery surface and can fly out of your hand, which is very dangerous for your opponent. Whichever grip you use, make sure it is dry. Always use a towel between points to keep your hands dry. If your hands are big, build up the size of the handle with wadding. There should be a 1cm (0.5in) gap between your fingers and your palm when you grip the handle.

COURT DIMENSIONS

It is vital to become familiar with the field of battle

A SQUASH COURT CAN SEEM QUITE SMALL, until you have to start racing from one end of it to the other in order to reach the ball. The secret of the game, therefore, is to force your opponent out of position, while remaining in a dominant position yourself. Spend a few minutes walking around the court in order to familiarize yourself with the distances and angles that exist in this unique area.

9.7m (32ft) Out line

2.1m (7ft)

MARKINGS

The red court-markings are found on the walls and floor. They define both where to stand when serving and the areas within which you are allowed to hit the ball. The serve, the first shot in any game, must hit the front wall above the **cut line**, before hitting any other wall. It must then rebound past the **short line** and into the receiver's box, before it hits the floor. If the ball does not reach the receiver's box, or if the ball goes above the **out lines** or into the **tin**, the server loses the **rally**.

9.7m (32ft)

1.6m (5ft 2in)

4.3m (14ft)

1.7m (5ft 5in)

6.4m (21ft)

FLOOR MARKINGS

You must have one foot in the service box when you are serving. If you win the point off your serve, you swap to the opposite box with each serve thereafter until you lose the **rally**, when the serve passes to your opponent. The junction between the **short line** and the **half-court** line forms the T, the central area that is of supreme, strategic importance.

WALL MARKINGS

The ball is "out" if it hits above any of the **out lines** or goes into the **tin**. A shot is also counted "out" if the ball hits the line itself.

DIMENSIONS

The principal target area is the front wall, measuring 4.6m (15ft) high and 6.4m (21ft) wide. The court is 9.7m (32ft) deep, with a full diagonal of 11.7m (38ft 3in). The side walls slope down to 2.1m (7ft), the height of the back wall playing area. All serves must reach above the **cut line** – 1.8m (6ft) above the floor.

6.4m (21ft)

2.7m (9ft)

4.6m (15ft)

Cut line

Out line

1.6m (5ft 2in)

Tin: 48cm (19in)

Short line

2.1m (7ft)

Half-court line

6.4m (21ft)

TELECOURT

The rise in popularity of squash in recent years has increased demand for spectator facilities at the major championships. Glass "goldfish bowl" courts have been developed that act like a one-way mirror so that the audience can see in from all four sides of the arena, but the players cannot see out. Adaptations have also been made to allow the television cameras to capture the excitement of the fast-moving sport, with special squash balls that are picked up clearly by the cameras.

• *The luminous ball stands out on-screen*

The game can be seen from all sides of the court

RULES OF THE GAME

The rules are designed to make squash safe and enjoyable

SQUASH IS A FAST AND EXCITING GAME, played in a confined area, so strict rules are vital to ensure safe and fair competition. Physical contact between players is inevitable during an intense contest as both struggle to secure positional advantage, but the rules prevent brute force from influencing the outcome. There are also regulations concerning the swing of your racket. However, the most important factors in making squash safe are consideration and common sense. These are especially important in social squash, because you will rarely have a referee. Both players must be prepared to exercise patience and restraint so that a vigorous and enjoyable match can take place without undue risk of injury.

• RACKET
An excessive follow-through could hit your opponent at head height.

SAFETY

During a game of squash, both players sprint around the court as they play their shots and also try to return to the T quickly. This means that inevitably, from time to time, they will get in one another's way. Close proximity also means that the racket, backswing, or follow-through of each shot could hit the other player. There is also a risk that players might be hit by the ball. These factors mean that safety is of prime importance. Each player must be aware of what his opponent is doing and where he is standing, in order to avoid contact.

ARM •
Use your free arm to keep you steady as you play your shot and prepare for the next one.

FOLLOW-THROUGH
An exaggerated follow-through is not only dangerous, it is illegal and could result in you losing the point if the referee judges that you were playing recklessly.

• FEET
Move your feet early to improve positioning and follow-through.

THE BASIC RULES OF SQUASH

SERVING

• A "coin toss" or "racket spin" is used to decide who serves first. The server chooses the box he is going to serve from, and proceeds to alternate between the two boxes until he loses the serve. The new server elects a box and also alternates until his opponent wins the serve back.

The server must ensure one foot is completely within the box

• A serve must reach above the **cut line** and land in the opposite back section of the court, although the ball can hit the side or back walls before it bounces. If it lands below the cut line or outside the opposite quarter, the serve is passed to the receiver.

• The server must have at least one foot inside the service box when serving. The serve must hit the front wall before any other wall – if the ball goes "out" above the front, side, or back wall, or goes into the **tin**, the other player gets to serve.

THE BALL

A player must make every effort to reach the ball

• After a serve, the ball may be played off any wall or walls, but it must always strike the front wall before it bounces on the floor.

• The ball may bounce only once on the floor. If a ball bounces twice or more, it is described as "down" or "not up", and directly loses the striker the **rally**.

• The racket can only make contact with the ball once on each shot. A "double" hit is illegal and loses the striker the rally.

AWARDING A LET

• If a player is prevented from reaching the ball or making a clean shot, he should stop play and ask for a **let**. If, however, he continues to play, or attempts to make a shot, no let is awarded.

• No let will be given if it is thought that the appealing player would not have reached the ball anyway, or if the player did not make a genuine effort to reach and play the ball. If a shot is attempted and missed, a let will not be awarded unless there was obvious **interference** on the opponent's backswing.

• If a let is awarded (or agreed to between the players when no referee is present), the **rally** is played again. A let will be awarded if a player would have got to the ball but was prevented from doing so by interference from his opponent.

AWARDING A STROKE

• If a **rally** is stopped when one opponent has played fairly and is in a clear, winning situation, a stroke is awarded. The player awarded the stroke wins the rally.

• A stroke is also awarded to the striker if **interference** occurs when he is in a clear, winning situation, or if his opponent fails to make a reasonable effort to get out of the way of the striker, ball, or racket.

• When the striker plays the ball and it hits his opponent, a stroke is awarded to the striker if it is clear that the ball would have hit the front wall first. If the ball would have hit the side wall first, a let is played. "Blind" strokes from the back corner that hit the opponent result in a **let**.

SCORING

• Games are played up to 9 points, with points being scored by the server only. At 8–8, the receiver may choose whether to play up to 9 points (known as "no set"), or up to 10 (known as "set two").

• Alternatively, games can be played up to 15 points, with both server and receiver being able to score throughout each **rally**. At 14–14, the receiver shall decide whether to play up to 15 or 16.

The ball may bounce, and make contact with the racket, only once

SHAPING UP

Strong muscles and stamina enable you to enjoy squash to the full

WHEN YOU PLAY SQUASH, you must be supple enough to reach for the ball; strong enough to generate powerful shots; and have enough stamina to see you through a whole match. The areas to concentrate on are your stomach, legs, and arms. A thorough warm-up before your game is crucial if you are to avoid feeling sore the next day.

OFF-COURT

Exercise off-court to get your muscles and heart strong enough for the games to come

FLEXIBILITY

Supple limbs are vital when playing squash. One second you are having to bend low to play your stroke, while the next you are having to reach up high. You will also find yourself sprinting around the court, starting, stopping, and changing your direction in quick succession – all of which is very demanding on your legs. Exercises that help to improve flexibility should form part of your fitness pro-gramme. Always jog on the spot for a minute or two before starting a game.

Lock your arms at the elbows and keep your fingers straight

Move in a smooth curve to touch your toes

TOUCH YOUR TOES
Stand with your legs about 60cm (2ft) apart. Hold your arms horizontally. With straight legs, alternate between touching your right toes with your left hand and your left toes with your right hand. Repeat 20 times.

Lift your leg onto a bench and straighten the knee as you lift up

STEP-UPS
Step up and down on a bench or box, about 30cm (1ft) high, leading with your right foot for one minute, then with your left foot for another.

BURPEE
Squat with your weight on your arms. Thrust your legs out behind you and then draw your knees back up to your chest. Repeat 20 times.

STRENGTH

It is useful to be able to hit with power and to have the endurance to keep going during a long match, so exercises that help to improve strength are essential. You should exercise for about one hour, two to three times a week to develop fitness and strength. Never neglect the warm-up exercises before going on-court, as these will ensure that the muscles you are strengthening in your overall fitness programme are fully warmed up. Exercising will make you stronger and more flexible, but don't exercise in order to become a body-builder. Muscles are heavy and if you acquire muscle bulk, you will simply have more weight to carry around.

Lift with your knuckles pointing at the ceiling, then turn them back

ARM PRESS
Holding a light weight in each hand, bring your arms up from your sides to a horizontal position. Try to complete three sets of ten lifts.

Stand with your legs about 15cm (6in) apart for this exercise

Hold your legs straight, with your weight on your toes

Keep your elbows clear of your body

PRESS-UPS
Lie on your stomach, keep your body rigid, and push yourself up using your arms. Try to complete three sets of ten press-ups each.

ROTATING SIT-UPS
Lie on your back with your knees bent. Sit up and alternate between touching your left knee with your right elbow and vice versa. Complete three sets of ten sit-ups.

Touch, but don't lift with your hands

Push your weight down to keep your partner's feet firmly on the floor

Twist at the waist as you reach for your knee with your elbow

ON-COURT

Stretching your muscles on-court before starting to play is essential if you want to enjoy good squash and avoid the risk of injury and stiffness

TORSO

Squash involves much more than merely using your hands and arms to hit a ball with a racket. Most on-court movement requires stretching and twisting of your whole body, so it is crucial to warm up the large pads of muscle in your shoulders and neck, your stomach, and your back. If you play without loosening them first, you could tear the muscle fibres when you make a lunge for the ball. The pain from this sort of injury is not only agonizing, it can put you out of action for weeks. Apart from risking serious injury, muscles that are not warmed up enough before use will not work nearly as efficiently as those that are.

• *Rotate your head gently in both directions*

NECK STRETCH
Relax the muscles in your neck and upper back before a game by rotating your head halfway in a clockwise direction, and then anti-clockwise.

Reach behind • *your head and cup your elbow in your hand*

ARM STRETCH
Pull one elbow behind your head and then the other, to stretch the back of your upper arm and shoulder, enabling you to swing more freely.

Keep the right side of • *your body on the floor as you lift your leg*

SIDE STRETCH
Lie on your back and extend your right arm to your right. Lift your right leg across your left one. Repeat ten times, and begin again, using opposite limbs.

• *Point your arm out flat and straight*

Hold your arms • *shoulder width apart*

• *Use your back muscles to lift yourself as high as possible*

BACK STRETCH
Lie on your stomach and lift your head, shoulders, arms, and legs into the air (only as far as is comfortable). Hold the position for two seconds and relax. Repeat ten times to warm your lower back muscles.

LEGS

In a game that involves as much running as squash does, strong leg muscles give you a great advantage. You need to be able to leap and stretch to reach fast and high balls. There are three main areas of the legs: the front and back of the thighs, and the back of the calves. After stretching and before vigorous exercise, it is a good idea to jog on the spot for a minute or two to loosen up your legs and body. Remember that you can't stretch your leg muscles too much.

CALF STRETCH
Lean against a wall and extend a leg behind you. Stretch the back leg by pressing down with your heel.

Push firmly against the wall for balance

• Put your weight onto your bent leg to allow the other one to stretch

• Steady yourself by placing your hand against the wall

FRONT OF THIGH
Balance with one hand against a wall and stand on the leg nearest the wall. Hold the ankle of your bent leg and pull it back. Swap sides and repeat with the other leg.

• Feel the muscles stretching as you pull backward

BACK OF THIGH
Adopt a half-squatting position, with one leg slightly bent and the other held straight. Move your hips back to stretch the back of the thigh of your straight leg. Swap legs and repeat the move.

Pull back on your heel •

Use your arm • for balance

SPRINTS
Sprint from one side of the court to the other. Touch the **nick** between the wall and floor at each turn.

THE WEEKEND COURSE

Understanding the Weekend Course at a glance

THE COURSE COVERS nine skills in two days. The skills included on the first day refer to the basic forehand and backhand ground strokes, moving on to the other essential squash strokes – **volleys, drops,** and **lobs** – later in the day. The second day teaches you the more sophisticated shots such as **angle shots.** Strategic playing methods, such as how to keep your opponent on the defensive while you try to **kill** the **rally,** are also explained. After the first day, you will be able to play an enjoyable rally. At the end of the second day, you should be able to engage in a proper match.

DAY 1		Hours	Page
SKILL 1	Forehand ground stroke	1¹/₂	24
SKILL 2	Backhand ground stroke	1¹/₂	30
SKILL 3	Volleying	1	36
SKILL 4	The drop	1	44
SKILL 5	The lob	1	48

Backswing for the high volley backhand (p.43)

Being prepared for the perfect forehand stroke (p.28)

Solo practice routines, using the backhand (p.33)

KEY TO SYMBOLS

CLOCKS

A small clock marks the start of each new skill. The blue part is a guide to how much time you may need to spend learning that skill, and the grey segment shows where the skill fits into your day. The clock does not indicate the time it will take you to apply any particular manoeuvre, but how much time you might spend practising each skill until you feel confident. Don't worry if you are taking longer than the designated times – they are just a guide.

RATING SYSTEM •••••

The complexity of a skill is rated by a bullet system based on a scale of one to five. One bullet (•) denotes that the skill is relatively easy to acquire, while five-bullet (•••••) skills are the most challenging.

ARTWORK ANALYSIS

The solid blue line (bl) and broken pink line (pl) used on the court diagrams show the flight of the ball: the (bl) is discussed in the accompanying caption, while the (pl) indicates a return or alternative shot.

Forehand angle shots from the front of the court (p.56)

Disguising the backswing for the forehand drop (p.44)

DAY 2		Hours	Page
SKILL 6	Wall shots	2	52
SKILL 7	Positioning	1	58
SKILL 8	The service	1½	64
SKILL 9	Rallying	1½	68

Using the walls and angles of the court to play across-court (p.53)

Hitting through the forehand lob (p.49)

Regular grip for forehand strokes (p.24)

1 FOREHAND GROUND STROKE

Definition: *Provides a range of shots, from power-**drives** to delicate strokes*

SQUASH IS A GAME OF POWER AND PRECISION. Of all the weapons in your armoury, the basic forehand is the most important because it allows you to hit the ball, either hard or soft, with great accuracy. It is also a shot that comes quite naturally to the novice player. Even if you have never held a racket before, you can still make a promising attempt at hitting the ball using this stroke. However, you should never take the forehand for granted; it may seem straightforward, but it is crucial to get this stroke right from the moment you start learning to play. It will be one of the main foundations of your game, so don't be tempted to proceed without mastering this skill first.

OBJECTIVE: To gain the winning edge with a perfected forehand. *Rating* •

— GETTING TO GRIPS —

REGULAR GRIP
Form a "V" between your thumb and forefinger over the top, inside edge of the racket handle. Allow your fingers to wrap around it to form a firm, secure grip.

"JAHANGIR" GRIP
Grip the racket further up the handle and turn it so that the top, inside edge of the handle moves to the right. This allows **slice** to be added to your forehand.

INCORRECT GRIP
In the above example, the racket is turned too far to the inside. This will mean that the face is angled, causing you to hit the ball either too high or too low.

BASIC FOREHAND

Preparation is the key to good squash. Make sure that your grip feels secure, and get into position early

STANDING FIRM

RACKET •
Keep control of your racket – from the top of the backswing to the end of the follow-through.

• **KNEES**
Keep your knees bent. This will make it much easier, both to move around the court and to inject more power into your shots.

As soon as you have played your shot, get ready to play the next. **Rallies** are lost when one player is caught out of position and does not have time to get ready for the next stroke. Always try to recover both the T and the ideal stance immediately after playing your shot. Remember that you can reach every part of the court from the T, without having to struggle. You may find it difficult to discipline yourself in the early stages but, with practice, it will become almost a reflex action.

FEET
Keep on the balls of your feet so that you can recover the T quickly and get your body into position ready to play the next shot. If you are caught flat-footed, you will lose the **rally**.

PRACTICE ROUTINES

FOREHAND DRIVES
Practise forehand **drives** down the right-hand wall. Start at the front of the court. Play high toward the back (bl), then move back and play the ball low to the front (pl). Sprint back and forth to develop a routine.

PACE & ACCURACY
To practise across-court, bounce the ball off the side wall or floor and hit it at just below knee height. To reach the back of the court, aim the ball high onto the front wall (bl). Concentrate on your swing.

1

DEVELOP YOUR FOREHAND

By adding power and precision to the basic forehand, you create a strong foundation on which to build your game

• ARM
Think "Racket back, arm up" and do both in one smooth movement. This will provide you with the ideal body shape.

Step 1

THE BACKSWING

For a good backswing, prepare early so that you don't have to rush your shot. Bend your racket arm at the elbow and raise it above shoulder height. Hold your free arm straight out, pointing toward the ball, and make sure the racket is held high. In order to adopt the correct position, maintain a straight line between the fingertips of your free hand and your racket elbow. Place weight mainly on your back foot during the backswing, but keep your knees loosely bent.

• EYES
Watch the ball as you strike it to ensure your timing is correct. Concentrate on hitting the ball in the centre of your racket.

• KNEES
Keep your knees bent. You are like a spring preparing to unleash its power.

• FEET
Put your weight onto your right foot. Use your left foot for balance.

Step 2

THE STRIKE

Bring your racket through a smooth curve toward the ball and "press" into the shot as you hit it (see opposite page). It is essential to be aware of the moment when the racket meets the ball, to enable you to play the shot accurately. To help you stay in control of your strike, try to concentrate on pressing the ball with the racket. As you hit, transfer your weight onto your front foot.

• LEG
Use your left leg as an anchor to help keep you steady as you pivot freely into the shot.

• RACKET
Sweep your racket through evenly and with power.

Step 3
FOLLOW-THROUGH

Never presume that your shot
is over just because you have hit
the ball – the follow-through is
crucial to the shot. Press the ball,
imagining that it gets stuck to
your racket as you hit it, so the
only way to set it free is by
pressing forward for about 30cm
(1ft). Allow the racket to complete
the second half of the swing, which
will send the ball in the desired
direction. When you get the hit and
the follow-through correct, the ball
will go where you want it to go. Your
follow-through should finish with the
racket head close to where it began,
as if you had drawn a circle in the air,
using the racket as a pencil.

• ARM
Keep your arm
loosely bent to
allow the racket
to sweep smoothly
through a full arc.

• KNEES
Knees should be bent
so that you finish the
shot as well-balanced
as when you started.

POISE
Be ready to recover the T immediately after
playing your shot. Remember, the mark of
the best player is not the single, perfectly
played shot, but the succession of good ones.

PRACTICE ROUTINES

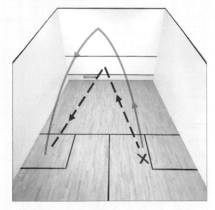

DOWN-THE-WALL
Play straight, landing the ball in the same
area of the court with a low, hard shot (bl)
as with a high soft one (pl). At first, just try
to land shots in the service box. Reduce
the size of your target as you improve.

ACROSS-COURT
Bounce the ball off the side wall or floor,
or play a straight shot before hitting across-
court. A controlled, softly struck ball that
rebounds high off the front wall (bl) will go
to the same spot as a low, hard **drive** (pl).

PERFECT YOUR FOREHAND

Practise with a partner to develop speed, balance, and the necessary technique for a complete range of forehand strokes

Step 1
BE PREPARED

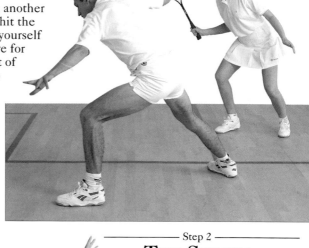

• RACKET
Remember the importance of the backswing – take the racket back high, in time for the shot.

When you practise on your own, you are in complete control. When you add the other important ingredient – your opponent – you will be battling for control with another player. As you begin to hit the ball to each other, give yourself plenty of time to prepare for each shot. If you are out of position or struggling to reach the ball, you will lose control and give your opponent the opportunity to take the initiative.

EYES
Whether it is your shot or not, always keep an eye on the ball so that you are not caught out.

• RACKET & BALL
The moment of contact between racket and ball is the most important in the **rally** – whether hitting or receiving.

Step 2
THE STRIKE

Whether practising with a partner or playing in a match, concentrate fully on the power with which you hit the ball, and the direction in which you want it to go. It is not enough just to strike every ball as hard as you can. You have to maintain control so that you can place the ball with touch and precision. Remember to press (see p.27) the ball as you hit it – this enables you to utilize your racket head to maximum effect.

POSITION
If it is your partner's turn to strike, watch the ball and be prepared to move as soon as it leaves his racket.

Step 3
FOLLOW-THROUGH

If you just stab at the ball, it is likely to travel slowly and in the wrong direction. Instead, use a flowing sweep to bring the racket head back almost to where it was at the beginning of the stroke, and the ball will travel directly to where you want it to go. Keep your wrist held firm to maintain control of the racket. Plant your feet wide apart to obtain a low centre of gravity, and extend your free arm horizontally for stability. Push off from the front foot to recover the T.

• POSITIONING
As soon as you have played your shot, return to the T, ready for the next one.

• RACKET
A high follow-through may feel exaggerated at first, but you will soon get used to it – and it has a winning effect on your shots.

FINISH HIGH
No matter how low the hit, the racket must always finish higher than your head. Never neglect the follow-through as it is fundamental to ensuring that your shots are accurate.

PRACTICE ROUTINES

HITTING TO A LENGTH
With a partner, aim at different heights on the front wall. Vary the pace to achieve shots of consistent line and length. Player (A) must turn his back to the left-hand wall to play a forehand (bl) across-court to (B).

WORKING THE CORNERS
With a partner, use the corner angles at the front-of-court to bring the ball back to the centre. After (A) has played to the left (bl), he moves to the T, while (B) moves from the T to play to the right-hand corner (pl).

2 BACKHAND GROUND STROKE

Definition: *Generates pace or delivers a delicate touch for a balanced game*

THE BACKHAND, UNLIKE THE FOREHAND, is not a stroke that comes naturally – it has to be learnt. It is, however, just as crucial as the forehand, so add it to your repertoire as soon as possible. As it is not always possible to get into the forehand position in time to make a return shot, it is essential that you are able to play equally well on both sides of the court; in doing so, you will also be able to exploit its angles. For this reason, you must work on your backhand until it becomes as easy a stroke to play as the forehand. You will then be able to play a wider range of shots from every part of the court, and will be well on the way to a fully rounded game.

OBJECTIVE: To gain a thorough knowledge of the backhand. *Rating* ••

GETTING TO GRIPS

REGULAR GRIP
Hold the racket at the base of the shaft. This allows the full, unbroken arc of the swing to be made, which in turn creates greater power in your backhand stroke.

"JAHANGIR" GRIP
Hold the racket further up the handle. This makes the swing "shorter", but it also gives you more control over the racket head; this can be useful when playing a **rally**.

SWITCHING GRIPS
Most players use only one grip, but if you need to switch, hold the racket at the neck with your free hand while you reposition your racket hand.

BASIC BACKHAND

*An effective backhand is essential because **rallying** demands that you are able to play good strokes from both sides of your body*

PRACTICE ROUTINES

BACKHAND DRIVES
Hit low and hard from the back-of-court so that the ball bounces at the front (bl), then move to the front and play softly to the back (pl). Go back and forth between shots. Keep the ball close to the wall.

TIME & PERSEVERANCE
Bounce the ball off the side wall or floor to prepare to play across-court. Aim hard and low (bl) to develop accuracy and control. A controlled swing and follow-through will produce sufficient power.

READY FOR ACTION

During a **rally**, you will be unsure as to whether your next shot will be a forehand or a backhand, so it is wise to adopt a stance that enables you to play either. Stand steady with your weight evenly distributed. Hold the racket in front of you and make sure your grip is firm. Concentrate on the ball and be ready to move swiftly to your left or right. Think about the trajectory of the ball, move to meet it, and strike. Then, most importantly, recover your stance for the next shot.

CONCENTRATE
If the backhand feels a little uncomfortable when you first try it, concentrate on hitting the ball in the middle of the racket. This also helps you to improve your timing.

RACKET •
Hold the racket in front of you at a 45° angle. If you hold it any closer, you restrict your body movement; lower, and it will be harder to make the backswing.

KNEES •
Keep your knees bent so that they are ready to propel you quickly to your next position.

DEVELOP YOUR BACKHAND

Injecting power and accuracy into the backhand helps you to
rally *effectively and, as you improve, to play attacking shots*

Step 1

THE BACKSWING

As with the forehand, the backswing
is a vital part of the backhand stroke.
Your shoulders play an important part
as you prepare to hit the ball. Turn
away from the ball, with the elbow of
your playing arm pointing down, and
the racket held almost vertically. You
will find that you are looking back
over your shoulder for the ball. Keep
your free arm clear of your body to
allow a full, smooth stroke and to
improve your balance. There should
be a smooth transfer of weight from
the back foot to the front foot to add
extra momentum to your shot.

• **SHOULDER**
"Give" your shoulder
to the shot. The more
you swivel your body,
the more power you
give to the hit.

• **KNEES**
Bend your knees to
absorb the transfer of
weight from one foot
to the other. Keep
your feet fairly close
together or you will
lose your balance.

HEAD •
Keep your head down. If
you lift your head, you will
hit the ball too high. Look
at the ball, not at the target.

RACKET •
Try to hit the ball
away from your
body, in line with
your right foot.

• **FEET**
Plant your feet about
shoulder width apart to
allow your body to turn.

Step 2

THE STRIKE

Many beginners make the mistake of
just slashing at the ball in an attempt to
generate power. Consider power later.
At this stage it is far more important to
concentrate on simply hitting the ball
smoothly. The point of impact should
be about 30cm (1ft) in front of your
right leg and about the same distance
from the floor. Press (see p.27) the
ball as you strike it; this will help
you to keep control of the racket
head in order to send the ball in the
chosen direction. If your swing feels
jerky or awkward, give yourself a little
more time to prepare for the shot.

Step 3
FOLLOW-THROUGH

Control is crucial when you play the backhand, because if you take a wild swipe at the ball, there is a danger that you could hit your partner on the follow-through. To maintain control, press the ball for at least 30cm (1ft) to give it direction and to keep your follow-through compact. You will also find that if you keep your arm relaxed rather than rigid, the racket will travel across your body to finish high and pointing up at the ceiling, as opposed to flat and waving dangerously into the open-court. Keep your eyes on the ball and your head still. Once your stroke is completed, return to the T in preparation for your next shot.

CONTROL
Concentrate on a full, smooth follow-through. This helps you to control the shot so that it goes where you want it to go. It also brings you back to a more upright position, from which you can recover the T quickly.

• RACKET
After you have played the stroke, your racket should be almost vertical. Quickly bring it back down in front of you.

ARM •
Keep your arm gently bent at the elbow. If it is stiff, you will be unable to complete a smooth swing.

LEGS •
Your legs should act as stabilizers until you have made your shot. All the weight is now on your front foot and you are ready to push off for your next shot.

PRACTICE ROUTINES

PLAYING STRAIGHT
Hit the ball to various heights on the front wall, but practise reaching a consistent length by aiming to bounce the ball on the **short line**. Pay extra attention to the high shot (bl), which demands more control.

ACROSS-COURT
Bounce the ball or play a straight **drive** to set up high (pl) and low (bl) backhand shots across the court. When you can hit the ball hard enough, a shot aimed just above the **tin** will bounce **deep** into the back-of-court.

SKILL
2

PERFECT YOUR BACKHAND

*Practise with a partner to develop speed, balance, and technique,
for a complete range of backhand shots*

RACKET
Your racket has to travel
far before it hits the
ball, so time your
swing correctly.

Step 1
PREPARATION

The backhand is not as natural a shot
to play as the forehand, so it is most
important that you allow plenty
of time to prepare for it. Turn the
shoulder of your racket arm toward
the front wall, bend your arm at the
elbow, and hold your racket up high.
From this position, you are able to
generate maximum power. Consider
where you need to stand
in order to produce a full,
smooth swing and a clean
contact with the ball.

STANCE
Twist your body as much as
you can so that you are able
to swing the racket with speed
and so give power to your shot.

Step 2
THE STRIKE

It is more important to control your
racket than to generate power. Hold
the racket firmly in front of you as
you make contact with the ball. Your
arm should now be slightly bent
and your wrist supple enough to
whip the racket through the hit.
Once you are confident that your
timing is correct, start increasing
the speed of your
strokes until you
are striking the ball
with great power.

CONTROL
Keep the swing as smooth
and controlled as possible.
Erratic movements will
adversely affect the pace
and direction of the shot.

• EYES
You will only connect
correctly with the ball by
keeping your eyes fixed
on the path of its flight.

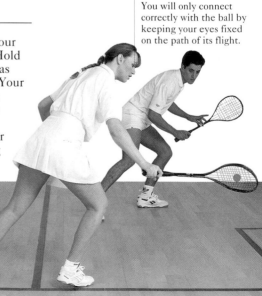

Step 3
FOLLOW-THROUGH

Completing the follow-through on the backhand is vital if you are to perfect the stroke. Pull out of the backswing too soon and you will lose power and accuracy – try it and see. To bring the racket smoothly through the stroke, turn your shoulders so that your body swivels toward the front of the court. Swing your racket arm as far behind you as it will go; this will allow your racket to finish high. Hold your wrist firm so that you remain in command of the racket head, which should be higher than your shoulder. Control the follow-through so that your racket does not lash out at your partner.

• RACKET
The racket head should finish high and point upward. Once the stroke is complete, prepare yourself for the next one.

MOBILITY
It is important to keep some bounce in your knees at all times so that you are ready to return quickly to the T in preparation for the next shot.

PRACTICE ROUTINES

HITTING TO A LENGTH
With a partner, hit across-court. Player (A) should hit low and hard (bl), while player (B) should hit high and soft (pl). Player (B), on the right-hand side of the court, should have his back to the right-hand wall.

WORKING THE CORNERS
Use the front corners to bring the ball back to the centre. Player (A) should hit to the right-hand corner (bl) then move to the T, while player (B) should move forward and play to the left (pl). Develop a routine.

3

VOLLEYING

Definition: *Striking the ball before it bounces on the floor*

THE ABILITY TO HIT THE BALL before it bounces on the floor is crucial to playing good squash. **Volleying** – taking the ball "on the fly" – is necessary, for example, when you are on the T and want to intercept your opponent's **drive** toward the back of the court. The volley shot allows you to play the ball early and thus seize the initiative. You can also use this stroke to attack, or to gain time in which to improve your defence. The earlier you play the ball, the more difficult the shot becomes for your opponent, so get into position quickly. When you first practise volleying, you may find yourself swiping at thin air, but persevere: an effective volley will enable you to develop well beyond the basic level.

OBJECTIVE: To play the ball at the earliest opportunity. *Rating* ••••

FOREHAND VOLLEY

This shot can be powerful or delicate. In either case, it is vital to keep a smooth racket action

• **RACKET**
Keep your racket head held high so that even with a short backswing you can whip up sufficient power for the **volley**.

———— Step 1 ————

THE BACKSWING

The preparation for the **volley** backswing is similar to that for a forehand **drive**, but because the volley is played before the ball bounces, you will not have time to take the racket back so far. To compensate, generate power by straightening your racket arm at the elbow as you strike, and direct the shot by using a **flick** of your wrist. The ball will be higher for a volley, so you may need to adjust your swing, but ensure you follow-through properly.

• **LEGS**
Plant legs apart to gain a lower centre of gravity. Keep some bounce in your knees so you are ready to sprint.

• **FEET**
As you prepare to hit, move your weight from your back foot to your front foot. Stay on the balls of your feet.

Steps 2 & 3
HITTING THROUGH

A well-played **volley** is a "meaty" shot that uses the full spring of your racket strings. Concentrate on striking the ball in the centre of the racket to gain power and control. Remember to press it as you make contact. Allow your weight to move forward as you hit the ball, to give extra impetus to the shot – essential because of the shortened backswing. By playing the volley shot, you will have speeded up the **rally**, so quickly recover your position on the T.

ARM
Point your arm at the left-wall **nick**. This opens up the front of your body and so allows a full, smooth swing.

STRIKE
Take the ball slightly in front of you and press it on contact. Use a **flick** of your wrist to give it direction.

EYES
To preserve your balance, focus on the point where your racket hits the ball.

FOREHAND

FINISHING
As you follow through, keep the racket head flat so that it finishes in front of – not over – your left shoulder.

Practise hitting forehand **volleys** to various parts of the court at different speeds. In a match, a cross-court shot to the back corner (bl) will force your opponent out of position and give you time to recover the T. Aiming low on the front wall (pl) can win you the **rally**.

SKILL
3

BACKHAND VOLLEY

To be confident on both wings, you must learn to play the
*backhand **volley** as smoothly and efficiently as the forehand*

Steps 1 & 2
PREPARE AND STRIKE

BACKSWING
Hold your racket
and elbow high and
away from your
chest so that
your shoulder
almost touches
your chin.

The backhand **volley** requires great
flexibility in the upper body. Swivel
at the waist and turn so that your right
shoulder faces the front wall. Draw
the racket back high, rather than
have it pointing along your spine to
the floor, and keep your right elbow
up and away from your chest. Put your
weight onto your left foot and use
your right to balance. Position yourself
so that you have room to swing your
arm and racket in one smooth curve.
Bring your weight forward onto both
feet as you play the
shot. Use your free
arm to help you
maintain balance.

— *BACKHAND* —

The down-the-wall **volley** is a useful
rally shot. It is most effective if the ball
"clings" to the wall all the way to the
back corner (bl) . This makes it hard for
your opponent to intercept, and adds to
the difficulties of playing an attacking,
return shot from the back of the court.

• **ARM**
Hold your arm
straight as you
strike the ball.
Your wrist must
be held firm to
keep control.

• **FEET**
Start with
most of your
weight on
your left foot.

THE HIT
Watch the ball as it hits
your strings, and press it as you return the
shot. Hold your wrist and elbow in a
straight line, parallel to the floor.

Step 3
FOLLOW-THROUGH

Perform a full follow-through as you spread your weight evenly between both feet. This smooth movement brings you round to face the front of the court so that you are ready to continue the **rally**. Don't cut your follow-through short in the hope that you will have more time to prepare for the next shot – this will only prevent you from controlling your **volley**. Although it is important to anticipate what might happen next in the rally, it is vital that you play each shot properly.

• EYES
Track the ball onto the wall. This enables you to prepare early for your opponent's return shot.

• ARM
Use your free arm to maintain balance while your racket arm is completing the follow-through.

• RACKET
The racket will finish behind you. Bring it back in front of you, ready for the next shot.

FEET •
Keep on the balls of your feet so that you are ready to spring back quickly to the T.

TIMING THE STRIKE

TRACKING THE BALL
The point where the ball bounces on the floor helps you to determine where it is in relation to you. Without the bounce, the judgement is more difficult to make. For the **volley**, therefore, you need to gauge the flight and speed of the ball as it leaves the front wall, and then calculate the exact moment to make your strike.

FEELING THE IMPACT
Make contact when the ball is about 15cm (6in) in front of your body. Press (see p.27) through the ball and try to feel its weight on your strings. This fleeting moment is your last chance to influence the direction and speed of the ball. The more you focus on the hit, the more control you have, but don't interrupt the swing when you hit – keep a flowing movement, with the impact simply being a point along the full curve.

• *Hit in the centre of your racket for power and control*

• *Keep your eyes on the ball as you hit*

• *Use your free arm to help keep you stable while you stretch*

• *Keep some bounce in your legs so that you can react quickly*

THE LOW VOLLEY

*Volleys hit hard and low make a powerful
attack and so are an effective way to win a rally*

RACKET •
The short backswing
makes it vital to press
(see p.27) the ball and
track it onto the strings.

——— Steps 1 & 2 ———
FOREHAND ATTACK

Any squash player will greatly enjoy
hammering the ball low into the front
wall so that it rebounds into the **nick**
between the side wall and the floor. If
you get the shot right, it is likely to be
impossible for your opponent to make
a return, but even if he does, he will
be in a poor position to retrieve the
next shot. To seize the initiative, play
this shot at waist level, from the front
of the court. If the ball is lower than
your waist, reach for the early **volley**
to rob your opponent of recovery time.

BACKSWING
Hit the ball slightly
in front of you, using
a short backswing. If
you strike later, you
will not inject enough
power and you
could also lose
your balance.

ARM •
Point out your free arm
for stability. Imagine a
straight line from one
hand to the other.

• LEG
Keep your
centre of
gravity low
by extending
your left leg
behind you.

— *LOW FOREHAND* —

Practise low forehand **volleys** into both
of the front corners. Try to make the ball
hit the front wall and then "die" in the
nick (bl). Even if the ball just misses the
nick, it is likely to bounce awkwardly
and so be difficult for your
opponent to return.

LOW VOLLEY
Bend your right knee to
get low. Since most of the
power comes from a **flick**,
keep your wrist loose. You
must get the racket face
right underneath the ball.

Steps 1 & 2

BACKHAND ATTACK

Use the backhand **volley** shot to intercept a loose, cross-court **drive** or a short, down-the-wall shot. It may seem a difficult shot to master but, as it can win you many **rallies**, it is well worth persevering with it. Take the ball as early as you can to enable you to maximize your backswing and to stay well balanced. Keep pressure on your opponent by playing a **short ball** into the corners, using the low backhand volley. Volleying gives your opponent less time to prepare.

— LOW BACKHAND —

One option is the **reverse angle**, where you play across the court onto the side wall first (bl). This is a difficult shot, but it can be very effective. The nearer the ball is to the front wall when it hits the side wall, the more difficult it will be for your opponent to return.

• RACKET
Bring the bottom edge of the racket through first to "cut" the ball low into the wall, making it drop sharply into court.

WAIST HIGH
Hold your wrist firm to press the ball home. Keep your forearm parallel to the front wall. Use the pace of the ball off the strings to give power to your shot.

LEGS •
Keep your legs apart for extra stability. Put your weight onto your left foot.

• EYES
Watch the ball as it hits the strings – in the very centre of your racket.

• WRIST
Hold your wrist firm, but keep it supple enough to allow a **flick** if desired.

LOW VOLLEY
Keep a low centre of gravity by putting your right leg forward and your left leg well behind you. Get into position quickly so that you can concentrate on playing the shot itself.

THE HIGH VOLLEY

*The high **volley** is the best shot to prevent a loose serve, **lob**, or high **drive** from reaching the back of the court*

—— Steps 1 & 2 ——
FOREHAND

As with all **volleys**, there is no bounce to help you gauge the trajectory of the ball, so concentration is vital. Think of the forearm action as similar to an overarm throw, but remember to keep control of the racket head. Use your free arm as a gun-sight to track the ball. The racket face is only at the top of its path for a moment, so precise timing is crucial. Hit the ball slightly in front as your racket travels downward. This will angle it onto the front wall.

• ARM
Whip through with your wrist, elbow, and shoulder, but ensure the hit is accurate and controlled.

THE HIT
"Throw" the racket head at the ball to make a powerful shot. To add extra momentum, turn to face the front of the court as you hit the ball. Transfer all of your weight onto your left foot.

ARM •
As you reach for the ball, stretch your free arm up high to help you track the ball and maintain balance.

PREPARATION
Point at the ball with your free hand, keeping your arm straight. Hold the racket vertical and your racket arm bent at the elbow. Put your weight onto the right foot.

FEET •
Launch yourself into the shot by pushing upward from the balls of your feet. Don't be caught flat-footed.

— *HIGH FOREHAND* —

When in the middle of the court, **kill** the high **volley** by angling it off the front wall so that it lands in the **nick** between the left-hand side wall and the floor (bl). When you are at the back of the court, play the ball down-the-wall or across-court to the opposite back corner.

RACKET •
Hold your racket so that its head is parallel to the floor behind your head, not pointing up at the ceiling.

LEG •
Use your back leg to push you toward the ball and to provide extra balance.

BACKSWING
Keep your racket face flat to maximize your backswing, and watch the ball closely over your right shoulder. Put your weight onto your back foot.

— Steps 1 & 2 —
BACKHAND

The backhand high **volley** can be an awkward shot to play, because you have to turn away from the front wall in order to prepare for the hit. This can make it more difficult for you to recover for the next shot. It is also harder to control the racket during the high, backhand swing, so concentrate on a smooth action, using your shoulder, elbow, and wrist. The high volley requires timing, balance, and accuracy but, once mastered, it will add winning skills to your game by allowing you to use attacking shots that prevent balls from reaching the back of the court.

WRIST •
A firm wrist keeps the racket steady. A final "snap" as you hit the ball gives it extra punch and direction.

UPPER BODY •
Use your upper body to reach and turn. Your arm cannot work in isolation, so move your body in one flowing movement.

THE HIT
To generate power, straighten out your racket arm from your elbow. Hold your wrist firm, but keep it flexible enough to allow you to angle the ball downward. For added power, transfer your weight onto your front foot as you strike the ball.

— HIGH BACKHAND —

The high backhand **volley** can **kill** the **rally** or place the ball out of reach. For example, the cross-court shot to the opposite back corner (bl) is useful when your opponent is at the front-of-court. Aim just below the front wall **out line**. Alternatively, play down-the-wall (pl).

SKILL

4 THE DROP

Definition: *A ball played near the* **tin** *or along the side wall*

YOU CAN PLAY THE DROP from anywhere on the court to catch your opponent out of position. If the shot is played straight, the ball will cling to the side wall. Played across-court, it will land near the **nick** on either the first or second bounce, making it difficult to return. The **drop** is often an outright winner, but even if your opponent manages a return, there is a good chance that it will set up a winning opportunity for you. However, the drop can produce unforced errors if you hit the ball too low. Give yourself a margin for error and try to hit closer to the **tin** as you improve. Do not over-use the drop, or your opponent will begin to anticipate your intentions.

OBJECTIVE: To play an effective **drop** that will force your opponent out of position. *Rating* •••••

RACKET
By holding your racket up high, you can fool your opponent into expecting a strong **drive**.

FOREHAND DROP

Disguise is important. If your opponent sees you are going to **drop***, the shot loses its effect*

———— Step 1 ————
THE BACKSWING

ARM
Straighten out your left arm to provide stability. Keep your knees bent to allow a smooth action.

FEET
Place weight onto your back foot as you prepare for the shot. Use your body to push into the ball.

Prepare for the **drop** as if you were going to **drive** the ball, by keeping your racket high. Your opponent will be unsure which shot you are about to play and will remain on the T. If you make it obvious that you are going to play the drop, your opponent will move to play the **short ball**. Balance is crucial because you need to control the strength of your swing so that you don't hit the ball hard. Plant your left foot forward and make a solid foundation with your right foot. Make sure your stance is correct, since a drop from an unstable position is unlikely to succeed. This shot calls for accuracy and control.

THE HIT

Last-second adjustments to the wrist can alter the direction of the **drop** and send your opponent in the wrong direction.

• RACKET
Bring the bottom edge of the racket through first.

HITTING THROUGH

Use the hit and follow-through to determine the pace and direction of your **drop**. Take the ball as late as you can to aid your **disguise**, but allow time to get your racket underneath it. If you strike at the ball from above, it will be harder to control and easier to put into the **tin**. Force the bottom edge of the racket through first to add **slice** to the ball. This will bring it down sharply off the front wall. Use your wrist if you want to change the direction of the shot at the last minute. Keep the follow-through compact. This will help you to play a firm stroke without hitting it too hard or too high. After playing your shot, you may find yourself between your opponent and the ball – make every effort to give your opponent a chance to reach the ball.

• ARM
Use your free arm to keep you steady as you follow through.

— FOREHAND DROP —

Practise straight **drops** from the front- and back-of-court. After playing a long drop from the back (pl), move forward to play a short drop at the front (bl). Angle the ball off the front wall so that it lands in the **nick**. The ball may miss the nick, but should still bounce near it.

COMPLETION
Keep your eyes on the ball to ensure that you raise your head which, in turn, will help you to balance and achieve a smooth follow-through.

BACKHAND DROP

SKILL
4

*Use the backhand to disguise **drops** played
either straight or across the court*

— Steps 1 & 2 —

PREPARE & STRIKE

Keep the racket high so that your
opponent cannot be sure which shot
you are going to play. Plant your right
foot toward the pitch of the ball and
concentrate on balance. The stroke
should be firm but controlled to
deliver sufficient, but not excessive,
power. Take the ball in front of you
and get the racket underneath to lift
it above the **tin**. Use a **flick** of your
wrist to change the angle of the racket
and so the direction of your shot. The
later you change this angle, the more
chance you have of deceiving your
opponent. Allow a margin for error
by aiming your shot well above the
tin. You will be able to hit lower as
you improve. Use the shot sparingly
or you will become predictable.

• RACKET
To prepare
for the hit,
point your
racket up at
the ceiling.

PREPARATION
Start with a high back-
swing and watch the
ball over your right
shoulder. Swivel from
the waist to turn your
back to the front wall.

• LEGS
Keep your legs
firm as you turn
the top half of
your body into
the shot.

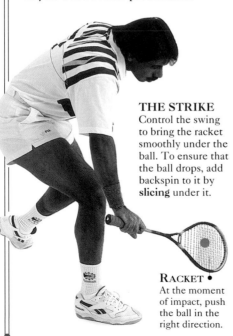

THE STRIKE
Control the swing
to bring the racket
smoothly under the
ball. To ensure that
the ball drops, add
backspin to it by
slicing under it.

RACKET •
At the moment
of impact, push
the ball in the
right direction.

— CROSS-COURT DROP —

X   X
A   B

With a partner, practise playing across-
court toward the **nick**. If (A)'s shot hits
the side wall too high, it will be easy for
(B) to play, so work out the direction
and pace you need to use to achieve the
"dead roll" from the nick. Aim the ball
just above the **tin** to allow for mistakes.

Step 3
FOLLOW-THROUGH

The follow-through must be compact as you press (see p.27) or punch the ball onto the front wall, but it is also vital that your stroke is sufficiently well-defined to give the ball pace and direction. Watch the ball as it leaves your racket and track it onto the wall. This helps you to stay balanced and ensures you are quick to return to the T. Keep plenty of bounce in your legs so that you are ready to push off once you have completed the stroke. Don't just assume that your **drop** will be an instant winner and simply stand there expectantly. It is better to be ready for a shot that never comes than to lose the **rally** because of poor preparation.

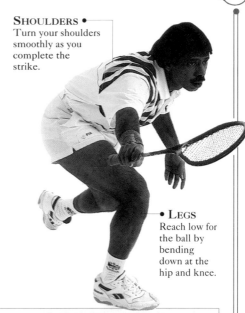

SHOULDERS •
Turn your shoulders smoothly as you complete the strike.

• LEGS
Reach low for the ball by bending down at the hip and knee.

FOREHAND DROP VOLLEY

When you **volley**, you put your opponent into difficulties because you take the ball early. If you can play an attacking shot like the **drop** volley, you will have an excellent opportunity to win the **rally**. To play the drop volley, move into position quickly and stay well-balanced. Take the pace off the ball by absorbing its power with your racket. Keep your wrist and arm firm, and apply a little punch as you hit the ball, to give it the necessary weight and direction – it is no good just sticking your racket in

the way and hoping the ball bounces onto the front wall. Aim high to provide a margin of error above the **tin**. As you improve, your shots will hit nearer to the tin. The bottom of the racket should go through first to deliver "backspin", which will bring the ball down sharply and make it harder for your opponent to retrieve.

Hold your arm straight out

• Bring the bottom edge of the racket through first to add "spin"

Keep your legs • apart for balance

SHARP DROP
Backspin makes the ball travel sharply to the floor. Aim for the **nick**, whether playing to right (bl) or left. **Slice** under the ball as you hit to achieve this effect.

5 THE LOB

Definition: *A ball played high over your opponent's head*

THE LOB IS A GREAT WAY to ease pressure and gain the initiative during a fast and furious **rally**. You can play the shot from the front or back of the court. Either way, it should force your opponent into a back corner and allow you to recover your ideal position. It is a shot that relies more on touch and precision than on power. Indeed, if you strike the ball too hard, it will either stray beyond the **out line** or bounce off the back wall into an inviting position for a **drive** or **kill** shot. On the other hand, if you hit the ball too low, it will set up your opponent nicely for a **volley** interception. However, when the **lob** is hit correctly, it can swiftly turn your defence into attack.

OBJECTIVE: To gain breathing space during the **rally**. *Rating* ••••

THE FOREHAND LOB

*Played from the front of the court in the same position as the **drop**, this shot changes the pace of the **rally***

--- Step 1 ---
BACKSWING

The preparation for the **lob** can look like that used for the **drive** or **drop** shot. As a result, your intentions can be disguised to keep your opponent guessing about which shot you are about to play. Plant your left foot so that it points toward where the ball will bounce. Turn your left shoulder so that you are almost facing your side wall. This enables you to turn into the shot as you play it and to use your right foot for balance. Keep some bounce in your knees to allow you to bend easily. Your racket can start out high, but get the racket face well under the ball at the moment of impact. As the stroke begins, open the racket face by turning your wrist until the racket head is almost horizontal to the floor.

• RACKET
Start high, but quickly open the racket face so that you can lift the ball from underneath. Try to keep your wrist flexible, but firm.

LEGS •
Place your weight onto your left foot and use your right foot to help you balance.

• **RACKET**
Open the racket face by turning your wrist. Press the ball on impact.

THE HIT
This is not a powerful shot, but you must play it firmly in order for it to reach the back corner.

HITTING THROUGH

In order to strike the ball to the back of the court without leaving yourself open to the **volley** interception, you will have to lift it over your opponent's head. To do this, get the face of the racket well under the ball and aim the shot about 45cm (18in) below the **out line** on the front wall. This provides height, without your having to use excessive power. The result, hopefully, will be that the ball drops gently into the back-of-court, where it is far more difficult for your opponent to make a return. If the ball rolls out of the **nick**, it will be impossible for him to return. A full follow-through helps the ball on its long journey.

• **EYES**
Keep your eyes on the ball as it climbs the wall.

FOREHAND LOB

Play the **lob** down-the-wall to the back corner (bl) of the court. Aim 60cm (2ft) below the **out line** on the front wall to get enough height to prevent a **volley** interception. The cross-court version of the lob (pl), if played accurately, should reach the opposite back corner.

FINISHING
Sweep upward to add height and direction to your shot. The racket should finish high, and over your left shoulder.

SKILL

5

THE BACKHAND LOB

*It is vital that you have the ability to defend by using the backhand stroke to play **lobs** to both back corners*

BACKSWING & HIT

• **EYES**
Track the ball to a point in front of you where it is just high enough to scoop upward.

BACKSWING
You can exaggerate the backswing to deceive your opponent, but for the shot itself, you only need to use a short, smooth movement.

• **LEGS**
Even when your legs are at full stretch, keep your momentum going forward to allow a full swing.

Use your body to help **disguise** your intended shot, and keep your racket held fairly high so that your opponent cannot be sure whether you will play short, **drive**, or **float** the **lob**. Move your weight onto your right foot and keep your feet well apart so that your centre of gravity is near the floor. Your wrist should be held firm, but keep it flexible enough to allow you to open up the racket face on contact. Altering the position of your wrist – using a **flick** – can change the direction of the ball right at the very last second, so enabling you to vary between using a down-the-wall, or cross-court lob. Hit underneath the ball so that you can lift it to a point high on the front wall, about 45cm (18in) below the **out line**.

THE HIT
Bend at the knee and waist to get low, and play the ball when it is in front of you so that you have room to sweep under it.

• **WRIST**
A **flick** of the wrist provides an extra push to the shot.

RACKET •
Get the racket underneath the ball to lift the **lob** up high and over the head of your opponent.

— BACKHAND LOB —

The cross-court option (bl) may feel more natural on the backhand than the down-the-wall shot (pl), as it allows a full follow-through. Aim about 60cm (2ft) below the **out line**. Hit various points on the front wall to see how the trajectory of the ball changes. Aim for the corner.

Step 3
FOLLOW-THROUGH

Effect a smooth and graceful follow-through as befits a shot that should soar high out of your opponent's reach to land safely in the back corner. So long as you have given the ball enough pace, it should reach the back of the court without hitting the ceiling or going out-of-court. Watch the ball as it strikes the front wall – you will have to crane your neck, but this is a useful discipline that helps to ensure your follow-through is sufficient to launch the ball on the correct trajectory and at the right speed. Push off in plenty of time to prepare for any return shot your opponent might be able to make.

BACKSWING
You may choose to exaggerate the backswing to deceive your opponent, but for the shot itself, you only need a short, smooth stroke.

• RACKET
Bring the racket through high on the follow-through to ensure that the correct trajectory is given to the ball.

HIP •
Bend at your hip and knee to help lower your centre of gravity. Be ready to push off quickly with your right leg.

FOOT •
Use your right foot as an anchor, but be ready to recover the T as soon as you have finished the shot.

BACKHAND LOB VOLLEY

When you are under pressure at the back of the court, the **lob** is a good shot to play, because it forces your opponent to the back of the court, and so gives you time to recover the T. If you can reach the ball early, play the lob **volley**. This is likely to gain you a winning opportunity. Get right underneath the ball and aim high on the front wall. Strike firmly so that the ball travels across-court to the back corner. Give your shot height to prevent your opponent from playing a volley **kill**. Take care not to sky the ball into the ceiling or above the **out line**.

• Hold your wrist firm

• Keep your legs apart for stability

• Use your left foot as an anchor

PENETRATION
Play firmly across-court to reach the back corner (bl), but not too hard otherwise the ball will go "out" or make an easy return.

WALL SHOTS

Definition: *Shots that use the walls to outwit your opponent*

SQUASH IS A GAME OF ANGLES. An experienced player uses the side and back walls to direct the ball where it is hardest to return, or to provide a route to the front wall that makes their opponent struggle. Watch what happens if you play a ball at certain speeds so that it rebounds at certain points. Fast balls behave differently to slow balls, and spin makes a real difference. If the ball goes into the corner, it can rebound twice. Once you are comfortable with executing rebounds, you will improve in both attack and defence.

OBJECTIVE: To introduce **angle shots** into your game. *Rating* ••••

REBOUNDS

*When the straight **drive** might be intercepted by a **volley** shot, use the walls to help the ball reach **deep** into the back of the court*

ACROSS-COURT

It can be hard to reach the back with a cross-court shot if your opponent is on the T. Using the side wall allows you to play wide and high so that the **volley** is no longer a threat. Aim for the corner, where the ball will be difficult to retrieve. Avoid rebounds that bring the ball into the middle of the court.

Open up your shoulders to allow the swing

AIM FOR THE CENTRE
Aim toward the centre of the front wall when playing across-court to the back of the court (bl). The further to the left you hit, the shallower the angle will be. This will cause the ball to rebound off the left-hand wall into court earlier than desired, and make it easier for your opponent to return.

BACK WALL & CORNER

If you play onto the front wall at an
acute angle, use the **lob** or play high
down-the-wall. If the ball strikes the
back wall first, and then the side wall,
it can be extremely difficult for your
opponent to retrieve. Similarly, if it
hits the back wall close to the floor, it
can be impossible to return at all. The
tighter into the corner you can make
the ball land, the better. Remember,
you will be punished for playing loose
shots that bounce into the open-court.

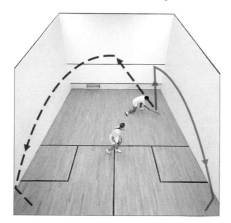

WIDTH & HEIGHT
It is essential to avoid giving your opponent
the chance to **volley** your cross-court shot
(bl). Width and height are the two means
of reaching the back of the court without
interception. If you hit high, use less power
to stop the ball going "out", or bouncing off
the side or back walls into an easy position.

DOWN-THE-WALL
When you play down-the-wall, angle your
shot slightly so that it clings to the side wall
(bl). This makes the shot extremely difficult
for your opponent to defend. The ideal shot
lands in the **nick** between the back wall and
the floor. Non-nick balls should bounce on
the floor rather than against the back wall.

—— USE ANGLES TO OUTFOX YOUR OPPONENT ——

THE THINKING GAME
A game of squash is not always won by
the player who simply hits the hardest.
Brain is just as important as brawn. Think
about where your opponent is positioned,
and use the angles to hit the ball to where
it will be most difficult for him to return.
Use touch and accuracy, as well as power.

DOMINATE THE COURT
The **boast** shot can catch your opponent
out of position, especially if you disguise
the shot to look like a straight **drive** or
cross-court shot. Use the time it takes your
opponent to return the ball to recover the
T. Even if your opponent does manage to
make a return, it is likely to be a poor one
that leaves him out of position, so you may
still have a chance to win the **rally**.

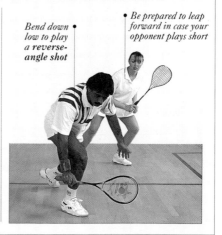

*Bend down
low to play
a reverse-
angle shot*

*Be prepared to leap
forward in case your
opponent plays short*

THE BOAST

Playing off the side wall first gives you attacking and defensive possibilities from both the front and back of the court

BOAST STANCE

Use the **boast** shot to either attack or defend. You must strike the ball with pace into the side wall so that it flies to the front. Adopt a similar stance to that for the **drive,** but face the back. This allows you to get your racket behind the ball in order to send it into the side, and from there to the front. The ball has to travel around two or three walls, so as well as using pace, you need to hit upward. If you hit the ball "flat", it will go into the **tin.** To help generate power, face toward the back-of-court, turning forward as you hit.

• **RACKET**
Angle your racket upward to direct the ball around two or three of the walls.

THE HIT

Play the ball hard into the right-hand wall. Even a shallow, upward angle will be exaggerated by the rebound on the side wall, so aim low to prevent the ball from bouncing into a position favourable to your opponent.

KEEP LOW
Keep the ball low to stop it from coming out of the front corner (bl). It should either die in the **nick** or be difficult to return. Hit with pace to force your opponent to move quickly.

ATTACKING BOAST

When you are positioned in front of your opponent, a **boast** to the front corner can cause problems for your opponent by making him travel from the back- to the front-of-court. Even if you are behind him, you can still play an attacking boast if it sets up nicely in front of you. For this to work, aim for the **nick** on the opposite side of the court. No matter how good your opponent's position, the ball will be almost impossible for him to return. Your shot may miss the nick and yet still be sufficiently difficult for your opponent to deal with. This allows you to regain the initiative as your opponent will be out of position.

TICKLE BOAST

The tickle **boast**, as its name suggests, is a delicate shot designed to drop low at the front-of-court – like a **drop** shot played off the side wall first. To keep the ball away from the centre, aim for the angle made by the front wall and the side wall. Play this shot firmly.

SIDE WALL
To carry the ball around the corner, play it firmly onto the side wall. This shot must be played with more pace than a **drop** shot, to give it sufficient height to reach the front.

DEFENSIVE BOAST

Whenever the ball has gone too far to allow a **volley** or **drive** shot, retrieve the situation with a defensive **boast**. You may have to play this shot when you are at full stretch or on the run, so balance is crucial. Hit upward with pace to get the ball to the front of the court. As soon as you have played it, turn to face the front and recover the T in preparation for the next shot.

BACKHAND RETRIEVE
Backhand retrieve **boasts** are useful when your opponent is trying to intercept a **drop** or down-the-wall shot. Aim for the **nick** to turn your defence into a dangerous attack.

Watch out for the •
defensive **boast**

THREE-WALL BOAST
When **boasting** from the corner, aim higher to ensure you reach the front wall. Angle the shot so that it hits the opposite side wall after the front wall to become a three-wall boast.

ANGLE SHOTS

*The walls and the angles they make allow you to choose from a wide
menu of shots in order to force your opponent around the court*

FRONT-OF-COURT

When you are at the front of the court
and your opponent is at the back, play
a short shot to make him run the full
length of the court, or pin him **deep**
with a shot to a good **length**. Make
use of the walls to cause problems for
your opponent by robbing him of the
opportunity to intercept. Wall shots
exploit the natural angles of the
court and prevent you from
becoming predictable.

*Be aware of your
opponent when you
select your shot*

FOREHAND OPTIONS

There is a useful range of forehand
options. The down-the-wall shot
(bl) should hit the side wall above
the service box, and then bounce
in the back corner. This makes the
volley hard to play and keeps your
opponent on the defensive. If your
opponent is standing at the back of
the court, the tickle **boast** (pl) (see
p.55) may be appropriate.

BACKHAND OPTIONS

Give your down-the-wall shot (bl) enough
height to reach the back of the court via the
side wall, without offering your opponent a
chance to **volley**. Don't hit the ball too hard
or it will bounce off the back
wall to make an easy return.

• *Use **disguise** to keep your
opponent guessing about which
shot you are going to play*

BACK-OF-COURT

When you are behind your opponent on the court, use the side wall to gain yourself some time to get into a better position. **Drop** shots can be risky, so only play one if you are confident of success. Usually, a shot across-court or down-the-wall – using the side wall to keep the ball out of your opponent's reach – would be the sensible choice. It is crucial to get height and width to stop the making of an interception that would probably lose you the **rally**.

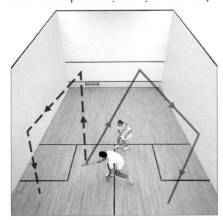

FOREHAND FROM THE BACK
Hit the straight forehand from the back of the court with pace, to force your opponent to the back. To prevent an interception, aim for the side wall, well above the service box (bl). The ball should bounce as near to the back-wall **nick** as possible. Recover the T as your opponent tries to make the return.

BACKHAND ACROSS-COURT
The backhand played from the back, across the court (bl), must be hit with sufficient force to reach the opposite back corner. This gives you time to move forward to the T, while simultaneously forcing your opponent into a defensive situation. Angle the ball into the side wall to prevent a **volley** interception.

MASKING YOUR INTENTIONS

Deception is an effective weapon to use when trying to outwit your opponent in the physical game of chess that is played out on the squash court.
The two keys to achieving **disguise** are:
• Making last-minute adjustments to your classic stance and swing. If you prepare for a powerful **drive**, for example, you can still play delicately by slowing your swing at the last moment and using a **flick** of the wrist to send the ball high to the back of the court, or to drop it short.
• Control – get your balance right and move smoothly. Use your body to mask intentions. Subtle changes of direction and emphasis, together with a good knowledge of the uses of the angles and side walls, will give you an impressive repertoire of shots. Plan out each shot carefully.

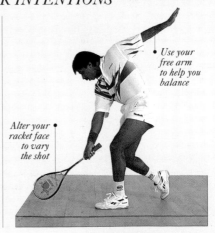

• *Use your free arm to help you balance*

Alter your racket face to vary the shot

7 POSITIONING

Definition: *Finding the areas from which to play winning squash*

A SQUASH COURT is only 9.7m (32ft) long and 6.4m (21ft) wide, but it can seem much larger if you are at the back of it when your opponent plays a **drop** at the front. You may cover the distance, but your energy will be seriously sapped. Remember, the best position to adopt as soon as you have played your shot, is back on the T.

OBJECTIVE: To gain a commanding position from which you can reach all parts of the court quickly. *Rating* •••••

DOMINATING THE COURT

Squash, like the game of chess, is a battle for positional advantage, but in this game, the winner is also able to dictate the speed and style of play

REACH

It is often far better to reach for the ball than to run toward it, as by the time you have got into position, it may be too late to make the stroke, and you will have used up valuable energy. The further you stretch, the more chance you have of making the return. Suppleness and balance are the two key attributes needed for this skill.

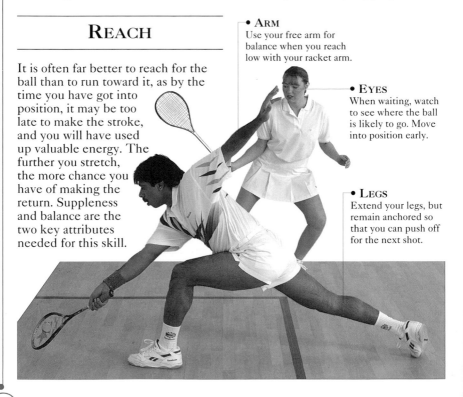

• ARM
Use your free arm for balance when you reach low with your racket arm.

• EYES
When waiting, watch to see where the ball is likely to go. Move into position early.

• LEGS
Extend your legs, but remain anchored so that you can push off for the next shot.

ACTION AREAS

Avoid playing shots that allow your opponent to hit the ball while he is in the middle of the court – the easiest position from which to win the **rally**. The majority of good squash is played near the side walls. The better the player, the nearer the wall most of the action will be. A central standpoint is essential to play this level of game. From this ready position, you are able to reach into each of the corners and intercept any down-the-wall **drives**.

SERVICE BOXES

Imagine that the sides of the service boxes extend to the front and back of the court. Virtually every shot should bounce between these lines and the wall – within the shaded areas. The nearer to the wall your shots land, the harder it will be for your opponent to make a return. Avoid hitting into open-court.

START FROM THE T

By always starting from the T, you should be able to reach the ball in just two or three steps, no matter which part of the court your opponent plays into. You must concentrate on returning to the T after every shot until it becomes almost a reflex action. Both of you will want to occupy the T, so get there first.

MONOPOLIZING THE COURT

THE BEST ATTACK
A strong opponent, player (A), will sense when you are in a poor position, player (B), and exploit the situation by sending the ball further away from you (bl). You may manage to return the next shot, but you will almost certainly be forced into a far worse position from which your chance of recovery is extremely slight.

THE BEST DEFENCE
If you are stranded at the back of the court, (B) there is a number of options open to the attacker (A), in both the opposite front corner (bl) and rear corner (pl). It is vital that you recover the initiative. Your best option is to play a defensive shot, such as a **lob**, and recover the T while your opponent makes the return shot.

Player (A) will capitalize on player (B)'s position

IMPORTANCE OF THE T

*The T junction, where the **half-court line** meets the **short line**, is the most advantageous position to be in for any shot during the **rally***

WAITING ON THE T

There are two players, but there is only one T, so the battle to gain positional advantage is crucial. You can defeat a player who hits the ball harder than you, just so long as your positioning allows you to intercept **drives** with shots that drop short or **float deep**. It is inevitable that you will sometimes have to move away from the T. At this point, it is vital to return with a shot that forces your opponent to move from the T as well. Think of each stroke as having three components: the preparation, which involves moving to, or stretching for, the ball; the hit; and the recovery, which involves going back to the T.

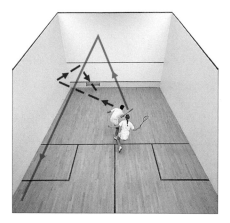

HIT TO THE BACK
When your opponent is "breathing down your neck", play the ball as far from the T as you can. Play a shot to the back with width, pace, or height (bl) to avoid the interception.

• **RACKET**
Get your racket under the ball to play the defensive return that can force your opponent off the T.

EYES •
When on the T, check over your shoulder for your opponent's position.

RACKET •
Hold your racket well up, in preparation for possible interceptions.

LEGS •
Keep your legs and hips facing forward as you look over your shoulder.

RECOVERING THE T

Your shot is not fully complete until you are back on the T. Assume that your shot will be successful and get ready for the next phase of the **rally**. If it is successful, but you have not recovered the T, your opponent may play a shot that you are unable to return because of poor positioning. Keep your movements smooth – if you lose your rhythm, your balance will suffer and you will be "wrong-footed" by your observant opponent.

SHORT-BALL OPTIONS

When you have to deal with a **short ball**, it is advantageous to hit it to the back-of-court so that you can return to the T while the ball is travelling. Aim down-the-wall (bl) or across-court (pl) and get away from the front wall – if you are hit by a ball that would otherwise have hit the front wall, you lose the **rally**.

CORNER SHOT

When you have been forced into the back corner, the best option is to play down-the-wall (bl) to regain the initiative and recover the T. This shot must be hit with pace to avoid an interception by your opponent, and should finish near the right-hand corner to force your opponent off the T.

DOMINATING THE COURT

CONTROL THE RALLY

To gain and maintain control of the **rally,** you need to be "fleet of foot" and "sure of arm". You have to be able to always reach the ball, hit it accurately and, if necessary, with power, and then return to the T. You must also be able to play **lobs**, **drives**, and **drops**, and be aware of how the **boast** can help you in certain situations.

TAILOR YOUR GAME

Most importantly, tailor the game to match the skills of your opponent. If your **drops** are always returned, stop using them. If your **drives** set up **volley** interceptions, use another tactic. Assess your opponent's position and choose the appropriate shot. For example, if (A) is on the T, (B) should play to the opposite back corner (bl).

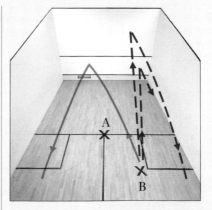

Play the shot as far from your opponent as possible

INTERFERENCE

Fast sports in confined spaces bring the risk of injury, but the rules of squash are designed to ensure that your game is safe and enjoyable

ILLEGAL SWING

Many injuries are caused when one player is hit by the other's racket. To reduce this risk, the rules state that it is illegal for a player to follow-through in such a way as to endanger his opponent. Remember that both players share the responsibility of ensuring safe play. Think about the type of shot your opponent is about to play and move around him so that he has enough room to make a full swing and follow-through.

• ARM & RACKET
During a full follow-through, the length of your arm and racket together is about 1.2m (4ft) – make sure your opponent is a safe distance away from your racket.

• POSITION
Don't tempt fate by standing too close to your opponent – it is you, not he, who will get hurt.

• RACKET
To complete a full backhand follow-through, keep the racket high and hold your wrist firm.

COMPACT STROKE

Excessive follow-throughs are the consequence of trying to hit the ball with power. In this respect, they are not only illegal but can be counter-productive, since a wild slash at the ball is likely to be poorly timed and will also fail to generate as much pace as desired. If your follow-through is not controlled, the accuracy of the shot will also suffer. Keep your swing smooth by pressing (see p.27) the ball on impact and sweeping through the stroke until your racket is vertical.

OBSTRUCTION

During a **rally**, both players focus on the ball and on returning to the T in preparation for the next shot. Inevitably, they will sometimes get in each other's way. A rally may have to be replayed if the **obstruction** was unavoidable. However, if you are seen not to have made a reasonable effort to get out of the way, the point will be awarded against you.

RACKET •
Obstruction, as well as physical contact, occurs when you cannot complete a full swing for fear of striking your opponent.

MOVEMENT

The direct route to the ball may be obstructed by your opponent, but it is important to make a real effort to go around him. It is unsporting to appeal for **obstruction** when it is clear that you could have played the ball.

RACKET •
If you have to move around your opponent in order to reach the ball, keep your racket well clear of him.

GO FOR IT
Make a genuine effort to reach the ball. It is important to try so that the **obstruction** is clearly evident. If you ask for a **let** on the basis that an obstruction could have happened, you might not be awarded one.

SKILL

DAY 2

8 THE SERVICE

Definition: *The first shot of a **rally** played from the service box*

SQUASH IS NOT LIKE TENNIS – there are very few **service** aces. The best you can hope for with a good serve is that your opponent will find it difficult to return, giving you an early advantage in the ensuing **rally**. Good serves rely on pace and accuracy in order for the ball to reach the side wall and, from there, the back-of-court. Once there, it is unlikely that an attacking shot will be made. Variety is the key to preventing your opponent from anticipating your serve.

OBJECTIVE: To force your opponent onto the defensive. *Rating* ●●●●

SERVING TO WIN

The serve is the only occasion in the game where you have the time and space to play exactly the stroke you want – take advantage of it

BACKHAND

Using the forehand serve from the forehand box can put you at a disadvantage, because you need to have your back to the receiver and must then turn to reach the T. However, you can solve this problem by using a backhand serve. It is a difficult shot to play and only really allows you to **lob**, but it is well worth having in your repertoire so that you can vary your attack.

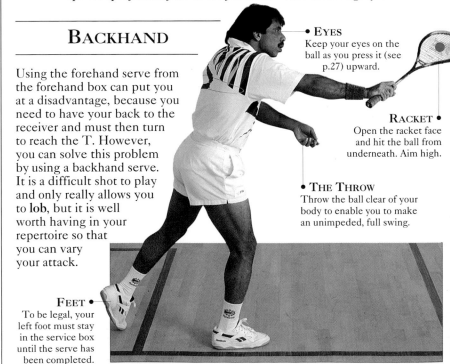

• EYES
Keep your eyes on the ball as you press it (see p.27) upward.

RACKET •
Open the racket face and hit the ball from underneath. Aim high.

• THE THROW
Throw the ball clear of your body to enable you to make an unimpeded, full swing.

FEET •
To be legal, your left foot must stay in the service box until the serve has been completed.

PRINCIPAL SERVES

Bring a number of serves into your repertoire so that your game is never predictable. Vary **drives** with delicate **lobs** and combine the two to "kiss" the side wall at the most awkward point – just behind the service box. Never angle your serve so that it travels toward the side at an acute angle. If it does, it will come into court where your opponent can make an easy return. The ball should finish within 60cm (2ft) of the back wall.

• RACKET
Angle the racket head to direct the ball across-court.

SMASH
Aim hard and low for the **nick** behind the service box. Occasionally, try speeding the ball down the middle to catch out your opponent.

• RACKET
Make contact with the ball once it is at head height.

WRIST •
Adjust your wrist according to the shot. Use a **flick** to give it pace.

SEMI-LOB
Play the shot firmly, but with a slightly open racket to lift the ball. Hit correctly, it should "kiss" the side wall, bounce off the back, and "die" behind the **service** position.

LOB
A **lob** can be unplayable for your opponent if the ball bounces high against the side wall to land gently in the back corner. Keep the ball close to the side wall to avoid a **volley** return.

SERVICE RETURN

*A well-executed **service** return can
offset the most accurately played serve*

RECEIVING

Just as a good serve can help dictate
the outcome of a **rally**, so the quality
of the return can determine who gains
the upper hand. Total concentration
is necessary when receiving, since the
server has the time and opportunity to
place the ball where he desires and at
his chosen pace. Position yourself just
behind the service box and watch your
opponent for clues about the type of
serve he is about to play. Always react
quickly and play an attacking **volley**
return whenever possible.

• SHOULDERS
Loosen your
shoulders to allow
for a forehand or
backhand return.

• RACKET
Hold the racket
head well up and
out in front of you,
in readiness to
return the shot.

• KNEES
Keep your knees bent
ready to propel you to
your next position.

POSITION •
Stand 60cm (2ft)
behind the service
box, with the leg
that is nearest the
middle of the court
on an imaginary
continuation of the
edge of the box.

THE KILL
To play the **kill** into the left-hand corner,
volley the ball down the side wall (bl). Aim
above the **tin** to allow a margin for error.

BACKHAND VOLLEY

The **volley** return can be particularly
effective if played before the ball hits
the side wall. Since the shot is played
so quickly, the server has less time to
return to the T and, therefore, is quite
likely to be caught out of position. The
backhand volley is difficult to master,
so the temptation may be to let the
ball drop and attempt to play a **drive**,
but then the advantage will lie very
much with the server. A volley, on the
other hand, opens up a great range of
options, such as a low, straight **kill,** a
down-the-wall shot, a cross-court **deep**
to the corner, and a cross-court **nick**
shot, all of which could win the **rally**.

FOREHAND ATTACK

Even if you don't have a chance to play the **volley** before the serve hits the side wall, you can still play into the front, right-hand corner if the ball rebounds in a position that is clear of the side and back walls. Alternatively, you could try **boasting** the ball to the front, right-hand corner. Either way, the server will have to leave the T in order to make the return, which will give you the opportunity to gain the upper hand. If you are confident at playing volley shots and so are taking most serves before they bounce, it can be effective to let the occasional serve just drop. This will prevent the server from anticipating your response.

HARD & LOW

Play your shot hard and low into the side wall to send the ball to the opposite front corner (bl). Your shot should ideally land safely in the **nick** or, at least, close to it.

FOREHAND DEFENCE

When your opponent delivers a good serve, you may be forced to play on the defensive. Aim to keep the ball in the air for as long as possible and to force your opponent **deep** to the back of the court. This gives you time to recover your position, and should also negate any advantage your opponent has secured. With your opponent at the back-of-court, play a shot down the right-hand side, or a **skid boast** to land in the opposite back corner.

Hit hard and upward into the side wall

HIGH BOAST

Counter a **deep** serve with a high **boast** that skids off three walls to reach the opposite back quarter (bl). Play upward and with power, to give the ball trajectory and momentum. Recover the T after playing the shot. Don't stand and watch.

• Remain in the "ready" stance as you check over your shoulder to see what your opponent is up to

SKILL

DAY 2

9 RALLYING

Definition: *The series of shots played in the battle for supremacy*

NOT EVERY SHOT YOU PLAY will be an instant winner. If your opponent plays a strong shot and gets into a good position, your only option may be merely to keep the **rally** going. However, if you are forced onto the defensive, your only hope then may be to recover with a shot that restores the status quo. It is a mistake to try to win the rally with every shot you play: you will make far too many errors. Rather, you should continue rallying on the defensive until a definite opportunity emerges for you to attack.

OBJECTIVE: To know which shot to play and when. *Rating* ••••

RALLY YOUR FORCES

Acquire a repertoire of solid shots to enable you to participate in a lengthy **rally** *and force your opponent to play on the defensive*

REACHING

The fewer the shots that get past you, the longer you will be able to stay in the **rally**. Reach for as many shots as you can while remaining on the T, and recover the "ready" position as quickly as possible. It is a good idea to practise playing a range of shots, using an extended stance from the T.

• **ARM**
Use your free arm to maintain balance as you play, and to help you recover the "ready" position in preparation for your next shot.

• **STRETCH**
Always try to avoid surrendering the T to your opponent. Whenever possible, reach for the ball, rather than move away from the T.

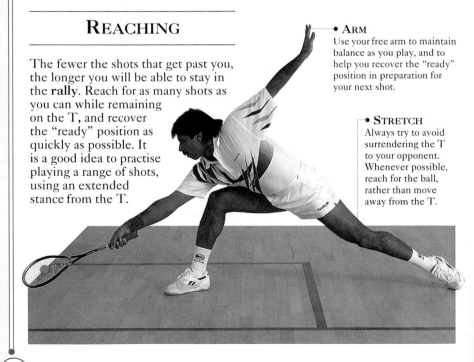

ANTICIPATION

When you are positioned on the T during a **rally**, your opponent will try to move you off it by playing into the corners. Try to anticipate where your opponent is about to place the ball, so that you can begin to move a fraction of a second quicker. This enables you to make a better preparation, and possibly create an opportunity for the **volley** interception. Bear in mind that players good at **disguise** can send you running in the wrong direction.

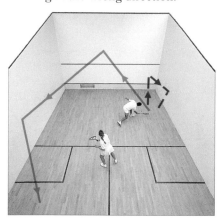

FRONT CORNERS
When your opponent is in front of you, it is difficult to see, and therefore judge, which shot they are about to play. You should be poised on the T, ready to move forward if they play a **short ball** – for example, with a tickle **boast** (see p.55) (bl). Don't always run to the ball – try to reach for it instead.

BACK CORNERS
A skilled opponent may try to outwit you by using the walls to send the ball to the back of the court. If the shot comes across-court, be alert for the opportunity to intercept it (bl). If the shot is well played, you will have to move toward it, but whenever possible try to reach for the ball rather than stray from the T.

PRESSURE

If you manage to succeed in forcing your opponent into the back corner, your position on the T should allow you to create a winning opportunity. You could have to deal with a cross-court shot, but your opponent may refrain from playing one as it can be risky. It is more likely that you will be faced with a shot down the side wall, which your opponent hopes will force you into the corner. Once you know this is the shot being played, intercept with a **drop** volley or a cross-court **nick** shot. This will force your opponent onto the defensive.

INTERCEPTION
Keep pressure on your opponent by looking to intercept the down-the-wall shot (bl).

CALLING THE SHOTS

*In every **rally**, you must think of ways to gain the upper hand –
always plan several shots ahead to outwit your opponent*

EYES •
Watch your opponent
for clues as to the
type of shot they
plan to play.

CONCENTRATION

Victory in a **rally** is often determined
by one player snatching the fraction
of a second that allows him to prepare
for a winning shot. Time is gained by
getting into a good position, watching
what your opponent is doing, and
then moving promptly to play the
appropriate shot. Always return to
the T once you have played your
shot, and continue to concentrate
on what your opponent is doing.
  Don't turn around to watch him
when he is standing at the back
of the court – you will lose your
"ready" position – instead,
check over your shoulder while
maintaining the correct stance.

• EYES
Track the ball onto your
racket and change the
angle of the racket head
at the very last moment.

SHOT SELECTION

The key to effective **rallying** is to
choose the right shot at the right
moment. If your opponent is
behind you, a **drop** shot may be
most appropriate. Alternatively,
it may be better simply to play
a continuation of shots to the
back of the court until a weak
return provides you with
a winning opportunity. A
variety of shots is vital –
if you consistently play
drops, your opponent is
better able to anticipate
them. Similarly, if you
always aim for the back
corners, he will remain
at the back of the court.

DEFENDING

When "pinned" in the backhand corner with your opponent positioned safely on the T, a down-the-wall return to a **length** is a classic **rallying** stroke to play (bl). Get the ball as close to the side wall as possible to make the interception more difficult and land the shot **deep** in the corner to make it harder to **drive**.

ATTACKING

Loose shots played by your opponent can be punished with attacking strokes. If a shot to the forehand corner is high and clear of the wall, it can offer a **volleying** opportunity that might allow you to **kill** the **rally** in the front corner (bl). Play a volley whenever possible to catch your opponent out of position.

REVERSE ANGLE

Use the forehand **reverse angle** (bl) to send your opponent in the wrong direction.

SEIZE THE INITIATIVE

When your opponent is beginning to dominate the **rally**, you have two options: play a defensive stroke that will give you time to recover the T, or play an attacking shot that could win you the rally. By mixing both types of shot in your strategy, you double your chances. Remaining on the defensive means that you will only win if your opponent makes a careless mistake. Combine low-risk, attacking shots with defensive ones to gain the initiative.

FIND THE WINNER

There are two ways to win the **rally**: either wait for your opponent to make a mistake, or play an outright winner instead. Winners are not easy. If they were, everybody would play them all the time. It is often much wiser to rally effectively until a definite opening arises. At the highest standards, rallies can last for many minutes as players probe each other's defences in search of a weak return. A popular tactic is to move your opponent from the front- to the back-of-court, using alternate long and **short balls**, in the hope that he misjudges the return.

AFTER THE WEEKEND

After learning the rudiments of squash, start putting them into practice

NOW YOU HAVE MASTERED THE BASIC SKILLS of squash, the best way to improve is to play frequently, against a range of partners. Join a private squash club or local leisure centre that runs a "ladder" system or league, where you can regularly play people of a similar standard. Every player you meet will have different strengths and weaknesses, so every game you play should widen your experience and help you to put your technique to better use. Treat each game seriously: get to the court in plenty of time; don't neglect your warm-up routine; and give maximum effort to the game. It is not fair, either to your opponent or to yourself, to play in a half-hearted fashion. Occasionally, in either your league or a tournament, you will come up against someone who is much better than you. This kind of match can teach you many valuable lessons about fitness, stroke selection, timing, and positioning. Concentrate on the factors that enabled the other player to win. If you do get thrashed, don't be depressed – everybody has to learn the game. If you play regularly, you should soon start winning more games than you lose.

PROFESSIONAL ADVICE
Watch and learn from better players. A professional coach can identify your weaknesses and point out mistakes in your techniques. Listen to the advice you are given, remember it, and then incorporate it into your next game.

PLAYING FOR LIFE

Sensible training and healthy eating promote good squash playing

•

NOW YOU HAVE MASTERED the rudiments of squash, it is important to find out how you can help your body to cope with the demands the game will place upon it when you play regularly. Playing squash will make you fit, but you should help to reduce the chance of injury or early exhaustion by respecting your body. If you smoke – stop. Don't drink too much alcohol. Eat a healthy, nutritious diet. Get plenty of sleep to allow tired muscles and joints to rest. These measures should help you to improve your physical well-being as well as your attitude to life in general.

AVOIDING INJURY

Never play squash if you feel ill or if you are troubled by an aching joint – you will only make matters worse. For example, if you have a cold, your body will be weak and so will be unable to recover from the exertion. If you have a painful joint, squash will aggravate the problem. Playing while you are not fully fit will, in the long run, only delay your ability to play further.

SHOULDER •
Violent swings can rip cold muscles in your shoulder, neck, and upper back.

LOWER BACK •
Reaching for low shots or stretching for high balls can pull your lower back muscles.

CALF •
Hamstrings can rupture when stretching for a low shot.

— TREATING INJURY —

A dull, mild ache is probably a minor muscle pull, which will heal naturally if you rest the limb for a while. However, a sharp pain in a muscle indicates a tear, which may be accompanied by internal bleeding. Apply a cold compress as soon as possible to stop the bleeding. Seek proper medical attention immediately.

A cold compress stops internal bleeding

STOP THE GAME
Don't play on if you suspect that you have injured yourself. Even with a minor injury, give the muscle every opportunity to rest.

WORKING FOR FUN
Working out in a gym is an enjoyable way
to develop all-round fitness. However, large
muscles impede mobility, so don't overdo it.

KEEPING FIT

A squash match can last for anything
up to two hours, so players need to be
fit. A sure way of developing stamina
is by taking regular aerobic exercise,
which, as well as improving muscle
tone, improves the body's capacity to
absorb oxygen, so enabling your body
to work more efficiently. The best
forms of aerobic exercise are brisk
walking, jogging, and swimming.
Exercise only becomes aerobic after
12 minutes, so you must continue for
at least 20 minutes. Aim to include
aerobic exercise three times a week.

YOUR DIET

You rarely see an experienced squash
player who is overweight. This is due
in part to exercise, but diet is also
significant. An athlete needs plenty
of calories, but they must be obtained
from the right sort of food. Fatty and
sugary foods such as biscuits, pastries,
cakes, sweets, fried food, and dairy
products should be avoided, or at least
limited. Preference should always be
given to foods that are low in fat and
high in carbohydrates, vitamins, and
fibre. These foods include
fish, vegetables, fruit, white
meat (without skin), pulses,
brown rice, pasta, and bread.

Fruit contains •
valuable vitamins
and minerals

Citrus fruits •
are especially
rich in vitamin C

Vegetables •
abound with
essential
vitamins

Fish is high in •
protein and
low in fat

Eggs are a •
good source
of protein

Pasta is high in •
carbohydrates
for slow-
release energy

Milk is rich •
in calcium

Pulses provide •
plenty of fibre

IMPROVING THROUGH COMPETITION

You will play better by playing better players

IT IS BEST TO AVOID PLAYING the same opponent all the time, because you will quickly get to know each other's game inside out, and so will find it extremely difficult to develop your skills. Play as many people as you can by joining leagues and competitions. This will expose you to different ways of playing the game, and provide you with ideas on how to improve your technique. Don't worry about getting beaten. In the early stages, it is almost inevitable!

JOINING A CLUB

Squash has increased enormously in popularity. There are now many civic sports centres and private clubs where you can play in pleasant surroundings at a reasonable cost. Most clubs and centres offer other sporting facilities too, such as a gym, tennis courts, and swimming pool. As well as allowing you to play squash with different people, joining a club will give you the opportunity to make new friends with at least one interest in common.

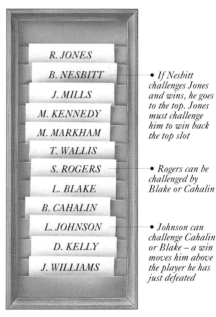

R. JONES

B. NESBITT

J. MILLS

M. KENNEDY

M. MARKHAM

T. WALLIS

S. ROGERS

L. BLAKE

B. CAHALIN

L. JOHNSON

D. KELLY

J. WILLIAMS

• If Nesbitt challenges Jones and wins, he goes to the top. Jones must challenge him to win back the top slot

• Rogers can be challenged by Blake or Cahalin

• Johnson can challenge Cahalin or Blake – a win moves him above the player he has just defeated

SOCIAL CLUB
In many clubs, you can relax after your game in the comfort of the bar. Some have viewing galleries, where you can watch others play.

LEAGUE LADDER
Most clubs run a "squash ladder". Such a system is designed to encourage members to play frequently in order to determine who is the best in the club. A typical ladder allows a player to challenge to a match either of the next two players above him on the ladder. If the challenger wins the game, his name is moved above the player he has just beaten.

ADVANCED PLAY

Notice how advanced players make top-level squash look simple. This is because they are fit and strong, they observe the golden rule of recovering the T, and they think about the shots before playing them. It is only when you come up against a player who is much better than you that you realize how important these elements are to playing advanced squash. But don't despair: with practice, determination, and a willingness to learn from others and from your own mistakes, you will continue to reach higher standards.

WINNING & LOSING

Whether you win or lose, just remember that nothing tastes sweeter than victory; nothing tastes more bitter than defeat. The wise player never lets either taste linger for too long.

TOURNAMENTS

The excitement of playing in tournaments will send adrenaline surging through your body. It is possible that nerves will ruin your match; on the other hand, you might thrive under pressure and become a professional competitive player. Either way, if you are good enough to play tournaments, you must take every match seriously. Your opponent will punish a casual approach. Get to the court early, warm up thoroughly, believe in your own ability, and give it your best shot!

SHARED TRIUMPH

My father is as proud of my achievements as I am honoured by his interest and constant faith in me.

TROPHIES

There are a great many competitions for all levels of player, each of which will award a trophy to the winner. If you are fond of silverware, get practising!

• *Tournament cup*

• *Annual champions' shield*   • *Winner of ladder*

RACQUETBALL

Fast and fun for everyone, racquetball is rapidly growing in popularity

RACQUETBALL IS EASY TO LEARN, but extremely difficult to master. You can enjoy the game the first time you play it, and continue playing for a lifetime without ever getting bored. The game's pace is frenetic, because of the lively ball, yet considerable skill and subtlety are required. Beginners develop an immediate love for racquetball because of its simplicity. The large front-wall "target area" is easy to hit, and the generous rebounds can help a novice stay in the **rally**. As skill increases, the methods of winning rallies become ever more sophisticated, with all the subtleties of court, racket, and ball being brought into play. Strategy replaces power as the crucial attribute, rendering mere brute force insufficient to guarantee victory. Like squash, racquetball offers the opportunity for both competitive and recreational play at every level. At all but the highest standard, it is possible for men and women to compete on equal terms, and children love the game because of its straight-forwardness. The game is suited to two, three, or four players, but the rules (see p.83) are relevant to a two-person game. Racquetball is a great way to obtain vigorous exercise in a pleasant, social environment.

A SPORT FOR ALL
Men and women, young and old, can enjoy racquetball. The equipment required is: appropriate shoes and clothing, a racket, a ball, goggles, and a glove. Kitted out with these, you can start enjoying the game straight away.

EQUIPMENT

The correct equipment ensures that your game is safe and enjoyable

COMFORT AND SAFETY are the two main considerations when it comes to getting the right equipment for racquetball. It can be a fast and furious game, which means measures should be taken to help prevent injury. It is also important to wear clothing that is suitable for vigorous exercise. As with every sport involving running, shoes are probably the most important item. You can select from a fairly wide choice of rackets and balls, but it is worth buying the best you can afford. Better equipment not only gives superior performance, but tends to last longer and so save you money in the long run.

RACKETS & BALLS

Racquetball was originally played with tennis rackets from which lengths of handle had been sawn off, but the disproportionate weight of the head made them unwieldy. This difficulty was overcome by designing rackets made out of much lighter materials, such as fibre-glass, aluminium, and graphite. The balls have also developed. You can now choose between the original non-pressurized balls and the newer and livelier, pressurized, rubber ones.

HEAD
The large racket head allows a margin for error when hitting the ball, but you must still hit in the centre of the face.

BALLS
A pressurized ball leads to a faster, game and so is suited to the more experienced player. The non-pressurized type is the best choice for beginners.

HANDLE
Choose a grip made of rubber or leather for moisture absorption and good wear.

LOOP
Always use the loop so that your racket cannot cause injury to your opponent by flying out of your hand.

KIT

The clothes you wear for racquetball must allow freedom of movement, and be light enough to ensure you don't get too hot. Items that retain moisture will become progressively heavier the more you perspire, and so should be avoided (see pp.10-11). Always make sure that your glove and goggles are comfortable before you start playing – constant adjustment during play is annoying for you and your partner. If your shoes are new, wear them around your home until they fit comfortably.

SHIRT •
Cotton is the best fabric for shirts because it allows moisture to evaporate and so helps to keep you cool.

LOOP •
Place your wrist through the loop and gently twist the racket until the loop feels secure yet comfortable.

• Use the headband to adjust the fit

Visors protect your glasses

SKIRT •
Pleated skirts allow women to run, bend, and stretch without being hindered. They also keep the wearer cool.

GOGGLES
Visors and goggles protect against eye injury. They should fit snugly, but not too tightly. Most have an adjustable strap to allow a comfortable fit.

Fingered gloves • offer good protection

Fingerless gloves • keep hands cool and improve "feel"

GLOVES
Racquetball gloves improve your grip by preventing moisture from your hand reaching the racket. The full-fingered gloves offer the most protection against blisters or chafed, painful skin.

SOCKS •
Cushioned socks help to reduce the risk of blisters. Cotton socks allow your feet to breathe easily.

RACQUETBALL FOOTWEAR

Wear proper racquetball shoes – the flatter sole reduces the risk of turning an ankle. Avoid normal trainers with a built-up heel. The raised heel may be useful for distance running, but can cause injuries in a game of sudden stops and starts like racquetball. Avoid worn soles, because these rob the shoe of its essential ability to grip the surface – skidding around the court is the surest way to get injured. Protect your racquetball shoes by wearing them only once you have got onto the court.

The sole of the shoe • must have a firm grip to prevent slips

The shallow heel • helps prevent injury

COURT & RULES

The dimensions of the court encourage a fast and exciting game

ONE OF THE BEAUTIES of racquetball is the simplicity of its rules, and this is reflected in the design of the court. Viewing galleries at the rear of the court often dictate how much of the back wall and ceiling can be used, but the basic shape of the court remains the same. There are no markings on the walls, and all of the walls and ceiling may be used during play. The markings on the floor are only employed during the serve and the return of serve. The rules are designed to allow a fast-moving game that balances power and skill, and which is safe yet highly enjoyable. The extreme liveliness of the ball means it can travel a considerable distance even when struck only lightly. It will also bounce very high, providing you with more time to play your shot before the second bounce.

DIMENSIONS

The court is a rectangle 12.1m (40ft) long, 6m (20ft) high, and 6m (20ft) wide. The back wall is always at least 3.6m (12ft) high. The floor markings consist of: the **short line**, which is midway down the length of the court and parallel to the front and back walls; the service line, which is parallel to the short line and 1.5m (5ft) from it, going toward the front wall; the service boxes, which are formed by lines connecting the short line and the service line. The service lines are 45.7cm (18in) from, and parallel to, the side walls. The receiving line – an imaginary line – is sometimes marked by two short dashes on either side of the floor.

QUICK & LIVELY
The liveliness of the ball means that most of the action takes place at the back-of-court. An apparently gentle hit can send the ball flying the whole length of the court, and back again.

• OUT-OF-COURT
Any balls that strike the 2.4m (8ft) top area of the 6m (20ft) back wall are considered "out".

12.1m (40ft)

2.4m (8ft)

6m
(20ft)

Short line

Receiving line

Back line

6m (20ft)

RULES OF RACQUETBALL

Main racquetball rules based on a game for two players. Up to four people can play.

All of the red floor- and wall-markings must be obeyed

• The server plays from the **service zone**. The ball must bounce once before the server may strike it.
• The server must ensure that the ball hits the front wall first, and then crosses the **short line**, before it touches the floor. The ball is allowed to hit the other walls before the floor.
• The receiver must stand 1.5m (5ft) behind the short line until the ball has crossed it. Neither the racket nor the receiver's body is allowed beyond this line as his opponent makes a return.
• Only the racket head may be used to hit the ball, and the player may make contact with the ball only once for each shot. The racket can be held in one or two hands.

• Unintentional **interference**, with the ball, or the other player, results in a "dead ball" hinder being awarded. This results in the point being replayed without penalty.
• Any interference with an opponent's play that could have been prevented, results in an "avoidable" hinder being awarded to the offender's opponent. If the offender was serving at the time, an "out" is awarded, and if he was receiving, a point is awarded.
• Unnecessary delays of ten seconds or more may result in a point being awarded against the offender.
• Unsportsmanlike behaviour, such as pushing another player, or failing to make a reasonable effort to get out of the way of either him or his racket, warrants the awarding of a point to the offender's opponent. If three penalties for this type of conduct are given, play stops immediately and the match is forfeited to the "wronged" opponent.

Swings must be controlled

Front wall

Service line

6m (20ft)

SERVICE RULES
The **service** rules are designed to produce a playable serve at the back of the court and so initiate the **rally**.

SERVING

The server stands within the **service zone** while he serves to his left or right. The non-server stands behind the service zone while the serve is made. A **drive** serve cannot be played down the side on which the non-server is standing if the server is within 1m (3ft 3in) of the side wall on that side.

12.1m (40ft)

1.5m (5ft)

1.5m (5ft)

Back wall

Front wall

6m (20ft)

Service line

Short line

Receiving line

45.7cm (18in)

GRIPS & STROKES

The correct grip and a repertoire of shots are essential for good racquetball

RACQUETBALL, LIKE SQUASH, is a fast game in which the ball travels at great speed around the entire court. To play well, it is necessary to develop a range of forehand and backhand shots so that you are able to respond effectively to rapidly changing situations. It is also important to develop both power and subtlety so that you are able to defend competently and exploit attacking opportunities. The foundation of any stroke is the grip. Make sure that the grip of your racket is comfortable, yet secure, and that you are happy with your glove. Practise alternating between the forehand and backhand grips until the movement becomes almost a reflex action as soon as you decide which shot you are going to play.

BASIC FOREHAND

Most players have a bias toward the forehand: it is the most natural stroke to play. There is a wide variety of forehand strokes from the low-power **drive**, to the delicate **angle shot**, to the defensive **volley**. In every case, the fundamentals are the same: you must watch the ball closely, develop a good backswing, and a full, smooth follow-through. Take the ball when it is in front of you to enable maximum power and control. If you take the ball later, you will have far less time to prepare for your shot, which may result in an unforced error.

GRIP
Shake hands with your racket so that the "V" shape (see p.24) lies on an imaginary line, down the centre of the grip. Wrap your forefinger around the grip like a trigger finger.

• ARM
When stretching for the ball, use your free arm for balance.

• LEG
Keep some flexibility in your legs so that you can move quickly.

• RACKET
To allow a full, well-controlled, backswing, the racket should meet the ball in front of your body.

• FOOT
Plant your front foot solidly so that you can maintain balance as your body swings into the shot.

BASIC BACKHAND

The backhand is sometimes seen as the weak side, and many opponents try to exploit this by directing most of their shots to that side of the court. It follows then that if you exercise to strengthen your backhand, you have a great advantage over many players. Balance is important, so prepare for the backhand as early as possible. This gives you time to produce a full, smooth backhand and to complete the essential follow-through, which gives you control over direction and pace.

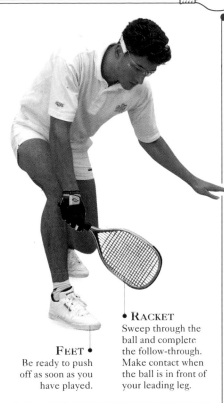

GRIP
For the backhand grip, first hold the racket as if you were about to play the forehand. Then turn the "V" shape toward your body so that it lies along the inside edge of the grip.

FEET •
Be ready to push off as soon as you have played.

• **RACKET**
Sweep through the ball and complete the follow-through. Make contact when the ball is in front of your leading leg.

CLASSIC DRIVES

FOREHAND
Use a forehand **drive** to play across-court (bl) or down-the-wall. Angle your shot so that the ball lands far from your opponent and forces her onto the defensive.

BACKHAND
A backhand, down-the-wall shot (bl) is a good attacking shot because, if played with the correct pace and angle, it forces your opponent to return with the backhand.

SERVING

*The opening shot of every **rally** can dictate who wins the point*

IT IS CRUCIAL TO ENSURE THAT your serve conforms with the rules (see p.83), and that it puts you in a strong position for the ensuing **rally**. First, master the basic **drive** serve, then practise a number of alternatives. Inject variety into your serving to prevent opponents from anticipating which serve you are about to use. In certain situations, it helps to be skilled at both attacking and defensive serves. For example, if an opponent is tired, a powerful serve that forces him to run after the fast-moving ball is the best choice.

BASIC SERVE

The basic serve is a low, forehand **drive** to the left or right. It should hit the front wall, close to the floor, and remain just above the floor until it passes the **short line** and bounces. Aim for the side walls to reduce the options available to your opponent. Move to the centre after serving.

• RACKET
Prepare your racket and body so that you are ready to spring forward as soon as the serve has been made.

ARM •
Use your free arm for maintaining balance while you are serving.

BASIC PRACTICE
Hit the ball hard to see how low you can aim and still make it reach the back of the court without bouncing. Shots to the left (bl) force your opponent into using the backhand.

BASIC SERVE
The serve gives the server time and space to prepare, free of pressure. Exploit this by concentrating on the backswing and follow-through, to ensure correct pace and direction.

ALTERNATIVES

Variations in pace and direction, and the use of the side walls can expand your repertoire of serves to provide a formidable array of opening shots. Practise on your own rather than during a match, as mistakes will be frequent while learning.

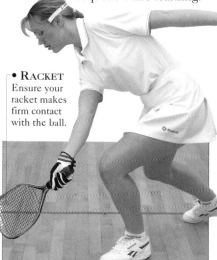

• **RACKET**
Ensure your racket makes firm contact with the ball.

ANGLE PRACTICE
Hit the **drive** serve so that it hits the side wall before bouncing. The nearer the back of the court the ball hits the side wall, the more difficult it is for your opponent to return.

ANGLE SERVE
The **angle** serve is played low across the court. Bounce the ball slightly further away from your body than normal, so that you have more space to angle your racket.

LOB SERVE
Play the **lob** serve with the backhand to force your opponent onto the defensive. Don't overhit, or it will make an easy return.

• **RACKET**
Sweep the racket upward to give the ball extra lift.

LOB PRACTICE
The **lob** serve should hit the front wall three-quarters of the way up it. Allow the ball to bounce high and get your racket under it. It should bounce twice before reaching the back.

SPECIALIZED SHOTS

A range of shots can be used to exploit the natural angles of the court

RACQUETBALL IS A GAME OF ANGLES. **Rallies** are won when a player sends the ball around the corners and out of the reach of his opponent. The essentials of any winning stroke are direction and pace, but this does not mean simply hitting the ball as hard as you can. Sometimes the slower shot proves more effective.

THE KILL

The **rally** is over if the ball bounces twice, so any shot played low off the front wall is likely to be a winner if it travels away from your opponent. Take your opponent's position into account when selecting your shot. Finding the **nick** between the side wall and the floor produces winners. For a promising **kill**, start with your racket held high and **drive** down to strike the ball when it is close to bouncing on the floor. You cannot be sure your shot will succeed, so always return to the T as soon as possible.

OPPOSITE CORNERS
When your opponent is to your right, play to the left-hand corner (bl). This means that she will have a lot of ground to cover and may be unable to reach the ball in time.

• EYES
Watch to see where your opponent is playing the ball.

RACKET •
Hit low into the corner to **kill** the **rally**.

CEILING SHOTS

The rules of racquetball permit balls to be played off the ceiling. This is useful in defensive situations where you need to force your opponent to the back-of-court, but want to avoid an interception. Don't play a ceiling shot if you are in front of your opponent.

• *Look over your shoulder*

Get under the ball •

UP AND OVER

If your opponent is standing in the **service zone**, bounce the ball over her (bl). From behind the **short line**, aim for a spot on the ceiling, 1m (3ft 3in) from the front wall. The ball will travel from ceiling to front wall, bounce in the front-of-court, and proceed toward the back. The nearer the front the ball hits the ceiling, the **deeper** it lands in-court.

ROUND THE WALLS

The lively nature of the ball means that you can send it across the full diagonal of the court without too much effort. Play this shot to force your opponent to the back, while you recover your position behind the **service zone**.

• *Concentrate on your opponent*

Direct the • *ball around the angles*

POWER AND PRECISION

When playing to the back of the court, it is important to deny your opponent the chance to intercept, if possible, so play with pace and ensure that you are accurate. Play off three walls to reach the desired area. Remember to move out of the way on completing your shot.

TACTICS

Brain is as important as brawn in playing quality racquetball

RACQUETBALL IS A TERRITORIAL GAME. If you can secure a strong position and force your opponent into a weak one, you give yourself the opportunity to finish the **rally** with just one well-placed stroke. It is crucial, therefore, to consider where your opponent is, what he is doing, and what he is likely to try to do, before deciding on your own tactics. Adapt to every changing circumstance.

POSITIONING

The best position is in the centre of the court, just behind the **short line**, which forms the back of the **service zone**. Like the T on a squash court, this is the ideal place from which to cover any part of the court. Much of the racquetball game is devoted to gaining possession of this area. Once you have obtained control of the centre of the court, use your choice of shot to gain the initiative and set the pace of the **rally**.

PLAYING AWAY
One way to stretch your opponent is to hit to the corner furthest from where he is standing. Use the angles of the court to direct the ball to the desired destination.

• **BE PREPARED**
When receiving, try to anticipate your opponent's shot. Keep your racket high. Move early.

RACKET •
Change the angle of the racket head at the last moment to disguise your shot.

• **ARM**
Use your free arm to keep you balanced as you strike the ball.

BACKHAND OPTIONS

The backhand can produce powerful **drives** or delicate **lobs**. Choose which to use according to your opponent's position, but inject as much variety as you can. Playing to the front carries a risk of errors, because a low shot might hit the floor first. Play **deep** to keep your opponent on the defensive.

HARD & LOW
A fast ball to the back corner opposite to where your opponent is standing may be a winner if it stays low or finds the **nick** (bl).

CROSS-COURT ANGLES

The ball travels at great speed without bouncing, so you can play it off three, or even four, walls. Such shots change direction several times, making it difficult for an opponent to find the right position to play a return. Use this shot when you want to pin your opponent to the back of the court.

CORNER TO CORNER
Hit hard into the front, right-hand corner and the ball will rebound to the back, left-hand corner (bl), making your opponent struggle.

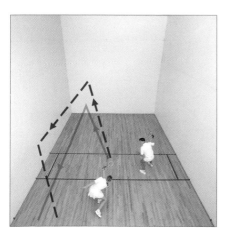

FOREHAND KILLERS

When your opponent is in front of you, turn defence into attack by pinning him to the side wall. He cannot move to the centre of the court until the ball has passed him on its way to the front, so if you play at an angle, down the opposite side, he will have to cover a lot of ground very quickly.

FRONT TO BACK
Hit the ball hard to bring it to the back of the court and prevent an interception. Keep the ball low to obtain the second bounce (bl).

GLOSSARY

Words in *italic* are glossary entries.

A

•**Angle shot** A shot played where the ball first hits the side wall and then the front wall, or vice-versa.

•**Appeals** A player may appeal to the referee or his opponent at the end of a *rally* if he thought that, during the rally, the ball was "down", "not up", or "out".

B

•**Boast** A defensive *angle shot* played off either of the side walls, or the back wall, onto the front wall.

C

•**Cut line** Red wall-marking across the front wall, 1.8m (6ft) above the floor. Serves must hit above this line.

D

•**Deep** When the ball is placed far to the back of the court.

•**Disguise** A technique whereby a player's movements and body position suggest a certain shot is to be played, but in fact an alternative shot is used.

Backhand drive

•**Drive** A powerfully played shot, taken low and with width, straight after the bounce (from about knee height), using the forehand or the backhand stroke.

•**Drop** An attacking, return shot that can be played after the bounce and off the *volley*. It is played with very little pace and should, ideally, be aimed just over the *tin* and close to the side wall to land "deadly" in the court or in the *nick*.

F

•**Flick** A shot whose pace and direction are achieved by flicking the racket from the wrist, rather than with a complete backswing and follow-through.

•**Float** A shot played high and with medium power is said to "float" to the back of the court.

H

•**Half-court line** The red floor-marking running from the mid-point of the back wall to the mid-point of the *short line*.

•**Half volley** A shot played a fraction of a moment after the ball has bounced on the floor, but before it rises.

I

•**Interference** Physical contact between players, either person to person, with rackets, or with the ball.

K

•**Kill** An aggressive stroke played hard and low to win the *rally*.

L

•**Length** Any shot that is played *deep* to the back-of-court is described as being played to a length.

•**Let** Where a *rally* has to be played again because a player was impeded.

•**Lob** A delicate shot that sends the ball high and wide over an opponent's head to land at the back of the court.

N

•**Nick** The area of the court where the floor and the sides all join. A ball played into the nick will be difficult to return.

O

•**Obstruction** A player is obstructed when he is unable to reach the ball or swing his racket freely because his opponent is in the way.

•**Out line** The red wall-marking that forms the upper limit of the court on all four walls. A ball that hits this line, or above it, is "out".

R

•**Rally** The period when the ball is in constant play, ending when one player makes an illegal move, hits the ball out-of-court, or fails to make a return.

•**Reverse angle** A shot played across the court into the opposite corner from where the player is standing, which hits the side wall first.

S

•**Scoring** Games are usually played to nine points, with only the server being allowed to score. If the score reaches 8–all, the receiver elects to either play up to 9, or until a two-shot advantage is achieved. Some matches play up to 15, with the server and the receiver having the opportunity to score from each *rally*. At 14–all the receiver decides whether to play up to 15, or until a two-shot margin is reached.

•**Service** The first shot of a *rally*. With one foot in the service box, the server must hit the ball against the front wall, between the *cut line* and the *out line*, to rebound in the receiving, service area.

•**Service zone** The area on a racquet-ball court, between the service line and the *short line*, from side wall to side wall, where the server stands while serving.

•**Short ball** A shot played in such a way that, after the ball hits the front wall, it bounces close to the front wall.

•**Short line** The red floor-marking running parallel to the front wall and stretching from side wall to side wall. It forms the front part of the service boxes, past which the *service* must travel.

•**Skid boast** A ball played to the side wall, high and close to the front wall, which then hits the front wall and lands in the opposite back corner.

•**Slice** Spin added to the ball by slicing the racket beneath the ball. Slice is most effective when playing a *drop*, because the spin causes the ball to rebound toward the floor at an acute angle.

T

•**Tin** The area stretching across the base of the front wall, 0.48m (19in) from the floor. Balls that hit the tin are "out".

V

•**Vibration absorber** A small disc that can be attached to the strings in the middle of the racket face. It helps to absorb vibrations caused when hitting the ball, and prevents them from being transferred to your wrist and arm.

•**Volley** Any return shot that is taken off either the front or side walls before the ball has bounced off the floor. The serve is therefore a form of volley.

Low volley

INDEX

GETTING IN TOUCH

Squash Australia
PO Box 356,
Spring Hill,
Qld.4004

New Zealand Squash Rackets
Association
PO Box 21–781,
Henderson, Auckland, NZ

ACKNOWLEDGMENTS

Jahangir Khan, Kevin Pratt and Dorling Kindersley would like to thank the following for their help in the production of this book:

Klaus Steed and Natalie LeServe for modelling.
Additional modelling by Sgt. Thomas Samms.

Mathew Ward, photographer, and his assistants: Christina Dormier-Valentin and Martin Breschinski. Emma Kotch and Linda Burns for hair and make-up.
Southbank Squash Club for the squash court.
High Wycombe American Air base for racquetball court and for lending equipment.

Olympus Sport International, Mr. Hamish Thompson of Reebok (UK) Ltd., and Willie Boone of Prince (UK) Ltd. for lending clothing and equipment.

Kevin Williams and Maria D'Orsi for design assistance. Colin Blythe, Sgt. Thomas Samms, Jane Poynden and Lesley Riley for proof reading. Hilary Bird for the index. Alistair Wardle and Alison Donovan for squash-court line artworks. Janos Marffy for colour illustrations and line drawings.

Picture Credits: Colorsport; Andrew Cowie p.15 (br),
Stephen Line p.77 (tl & c).
t: top, b: bottom, l: left, r: right, c: centre